Robin R. Lyons

WHAT'S RIGHT
WITH THE CHURCH

What's Right
with the Church

WILLIAM H. WILLIMON

1817

Harper & Row, Publishers, San Francisco

Cambridge, Hagerstown, New York, Philadelphia
London, Mexico City, São Paulo, Singapore, Sydney

Portions of chapter 7 originally appeared in *The Christian Century* under the title "In Praise of Excess," copyright 1983, Christian Century Foundation. Reprinted by permission from the October 19, 1983 issue of *The Christian Century*. Portions of chapter 8 originally appeared in *Quarterly Review: A Scholarly Journal for Reflection on Ministry*, Summer, 1983, copyright © The United Methodist Publishing House and the United Methodist Board of Higher Education and Ministry.

FIRST EDITION

Library of Congress Cataloging in Publication Data

Willimon, William H.
  WHAT'S RIGHT WITH THE CHURCH

  1. Church. I. Title.
BV600.2.W55 1985   262   84-48233
ISBN 0-06-069531-5

---

85 86 87 88 89   10 9 8 7 6 5 4 3 2 1

To Betty and Sinclair
who help make things right

Contents

Introduction   1

1. Where Is the Church?   7

2. Why the Church?   33

3. In, But Not of, the World   49

4. Acting Like Christians   75

5. The Bible: The Church's Book   92

6. Preaching: Hearing Is Believing   101

7. Common Prayer   114

8. Priests Everywhere   125

Epilogue   137

Notes   141

Index   143

Show me deare Christ, thy Spouse, so bright and clear.
What! is it She, which on the other shore
Goes richly painted? or which rob'd and tore
Laments and mournes in Germany and here?
Sleeps she a thousand, then peepes up one yeare?
Is she selfe truth and errs? now new, now outwore?
Doth she, and did she, and shall she evermore
On one, on seaven, or on no hill appeare?
Dwells she with us, or like adventuring knights
First travaile we to seeke and then make Love?
Betray kind husband thy spouse to our sights,
and let myne amorous soule court thy mild Dove,
Who is most trew, and pleasing to thee, then
When she'is embrac'd and open to most men.

—JOHN DONNE, *Holy Sonnets XVIII*

Introduction

THERE WAS once a man in Iowa who got married. He had long been enamored of the idea of marriage, so when he met "the woman of my dreams," he proposed to her. Things went well at first. He told his friends that his new wife was "all I ever hoped for in a woman." She was beautiful, intelligent, witty. His friends observed that here was "a marriage made in heaven."

Unfortunately, this initial bliss was not to last. Gradually, in day-to-day living he began to notice certain imperfections in his new wife. She was beautiful, but not always. Sometimes, say, before nine in the morning, she was downright unattractive, even ugly. She could look stunning for great parties and social occasions, but marriage meant that he had to look at her before she got her makeup on in the morning, and he couldn't help thinking of that more than her beauty. Yes, she was intelligent, you couldn't take that from her, but there were gaps in her knowledge, rather large gaps. She knew a great deal about a few matters, but there were many areas of interest about which she was as ignorant as the day she was born. This displeased him greatly. He knew there would be a time when she would embarrass him by making some ill-considered statement in public, thus revealing to the whole world her intellectual imperfections. This bothered him.

Slowly, but surely, he found himself growing cool to this woman. Marriage had proved to be different than he had thought. It had been fun to be with her on a Saturday evening, to dance with her into the wee hours of the morning at a society ball. But marriage wasn't like that at all. Marriage was corn-flakes for breakfast, and someone sleeping beside you with large curlers in her hair; it was disagreements over finances, and visits from her Oklahoma relatives, and that grotesque lamp that she had selected for the living room. That was marriage.

He still believed in love more than ever. He still longed for the perfect partner. He continued to cling to the idea of marriage. The idea was fine; it was the particular experience of marriage that bothered him. The man who marries "the woman of my dreams," the woman who marries "Mister Right"—each will discover that the particular experience of this person is quite different from the ideal.

A persistent danger in the religious life in any age is abstraction and universalization. It is the danger of the noble, abstract ideal—the appeal of the inner essence, the four spiritual laws, the great, all-encompassing truth. People are always trying to reduce Christianity to a set of abstract and high-sounding platitudes, grand concepts, generalizations, and inspiring visions. "The gospel is basically about love," they may say. Or, the message of Jesus is simply, "The fatherhood of God and the brotherhood of man." Christianity is simply about acceptance, or about serving others, or about liberation, or about freedom, or about whatever platitude happens to be in vogue. We do this because it makes Christianity easier for us to swallow. It is difficult to speak for other religions, but when it comes to the religion called Christianity, it's the scandal of particularity that bothers us. The thing that sticks in our collective craw is not that the gospel is about love, peace, freedom, liberation, or any other lovable abstraction. The gospel is a complicated story of a young Jew from Nazareth, Jesus, who lived, taught, suffered, died, and rose. Abstractions are appealing because they enable us to make Jesus anything we like. They are large, empty baskets that we can fill with more agreeable content. But there is little abstraction in the story of Jesus. It is the particularity of it all that is so striking. As you read the Gospels, you can almost taste the dust along the roadside, smell the stable of the nativity, hear the thunder of the mob. Your sight falls, not upon uplifting and inspiring visions, but upon mustard seeds, coins, lepers, spittle mixed with dirt, and an enigmatic young prophet whose words will not let you go. This is the scandal of particularity.

To be part of the gospel is to come to terms with this Jew, this people, this place, these words and events. The gospel is neither the sum of our highest human aspirations nor a beautiful story about a wonderful human being that mirrors the best and the brightest of all our stories. Many, indeed, have tried to make Jesus an example of the best within us, a kind of ideal person. They have failed, because the particulars of Jesus will not allow that. Many have turned away from Jesus and his way because of the particulars of the story. They are enamored of the idea of a loving God, in love with the concept of love. But the gospel is not so much ideas or concepts as cold particulars. It's the hard facts, the specifics, the little, solid words and concrete images, the simple commands that puncture our Sunday inspiration with Monday-morning reality.

What is said of Jesus holds true for his church. It is the scandal of particularity that bothers us. Like the man in love with love in my parable, fascinated by the idea of marriage, many approve of both the idea of following Christ and the concept of the church. But they are horrified by the squalid particulars. It was the romantic poet Southey who said, "I could believe in Christ if he did not drag behind him his leprous bride, the Church." Jesus has many admirers who feel that he married beneath his station. They love Christ but are unable to love those whom he has loved.

For these admirers, Jesus is best followed in the safe confines of their own living rooms through a religious program on the television, or by thinking noble thoughts about God in the privacy of their library, or by pleasant conversation with someone else who sees things the same way. Jesus is fine. It's those people of Jesus, that contentious crowd at Saint John's of the Expressway, that bother them.

thesis!

This is a book about the church that assumes that the chief scandal of the church is its particularity, its incarnational quality. This is my attempt to think about the church by focusing on some of its specifics as I have experienced them. Therefore, I think about the church, not by starting with definitions of its inner essence or outer characteristics, but by looking at episodes, stories in the life of churches, from my own experience. I assume that the way to know about the church is to know it in the flesh, as it is. Frankly, this is the only way to know the church, just as particulars are the only way to know Jesus. The only church we ever know is the one that happens in history, in the flesh. To know something else is to know something that doesn't exist, a projection of our own fantasies of what we would like to be rather than what is.

By beginning with my experience of the church, I am assuming that your experience is similar enough to make what I say relevant. One of the things preachers sometimes discover is that, by focusing as concretely and particularly as you can upon your faith journey, you often succeed in linking your experiences with those of others, not by generalization but by particularization. It is difficult to be universal without also being provincial.

Throughout this book I shall use traditional and contemporary sources for thinking about the church, as a means of helping me reflect upon my own experiences. Biblical testimony on the church will be important. In using biblical data, we are not moving from the particular to the general and abstract. As noted earlier, the Bible's treatment of the church is characterized by preoccupation with the little, day-to-day concerns of particular congregations rather than speculation or undue concern about defining the essence or meaning of the universal church.

Paul is unconcerned with speculation on the real meaning of the church, a doctrine that must then be put into practice. Paul begins with the church as it happens, as a fact. Mostly, Paul's thought on the church arises the way any pastor thinks: trying to put out a fire among the board at Corinth, putting a few upstarts in their place in Galatia, giving a little encouragement to the disheartened saints at Philippi.

The New Testament itself is a response to the earliest identity crises of the church. In using the New Testament as our model for thinking about the church, we are continuing the process of self-reflection, self-criticism, and self-discovery that it began. We do not defer to these scriptural sources out of some notion that the church was then pure but out of our need always to return to our origins, not in time, but in substance.

I decided to write this book because I have noted that my thinking in the past few years has become increasingly concerned with ecclesiology. In one way or another, my books on worship, preaching, ethics, and Christian education turn out to be books about the church. By my informal count, there have been over one hundred books on the church published by the major, mainline religious publishing houses in the past two decades.

Books about the church seem to come in cycles. Very few works in ecclesiology were published in the decades before and after the turn of the century. There were a great number in the pre–World War II years, then a veritable avalanche since 1960. Perhaps the church thinks about itself only when it has to— when forces demand that the church rethink who it is, whose it is, and what it is supposed to be and be doing. Our age continues to be such a time. The church that is reformed and ever reforming is called to rethink what conditions make the church and how we are to be faithful in this time and place.

Fortunately, we have had a number of solid theological and biblical studies of the church in the years since Vatican II. The works of people like Karl Barth, Hans Küng, and Edward Shillebeeckx come to mind. This book attempts to build upon their conclusions in focusing upon particular experiences within a mainline Protestant denomination in North America and letting these experiences enrich and illustrate current thought about the church.

Since writing this book, I have moved from the pastorate of a congregation in Greenville, South Carolina, to the pastorate of a university chapel. While I continue to preach and to perform pastoral duties, my congregation here at Duke University is different from those where most Christians work and worship and unlike the churches that led me to write this book. Yet now, as a minister and a professor of ministry at a university, I see from a distance that which I experienced close-up: The Christian faith's most basic unit is the congregation. This book is my love song to and my lover's quarrel with those congregations.

These thoughts began with a hunch that has grown into a basic belief: There is no more important task for the Christian who is called to be a pastor than to help the church think about the church. The unique vocation of the pastor, I will argue later, is to be the "community person," the one who helps the church to be the church. Take the following pages as this pastor's struggle to fulfill that vocation.

1. Where Is the Church?

THE BISHOP has appointed me to a church that is difficult to find. The congregation planned to be on the outskirts of the city, the cutting edge of Greenville's northward move. North-side Church was the rather unpretentious name it gave itself. But like many neighborhood churches, Northside stopped growing as the city continued beyond its northern boundaries, miles past us, as farms became subdivisions and a dozen new congregations were formed to enjoy the benefits of expanding suburbia. Today the church would more appropriately call itself City Center rather than Northside. We have become a five-hundred-member congregation in an aging neighborhood. Summit Drive, which was to be the main artery for traffic to the city's northern limits, has become a quiet street with few pas-sersby. Not one Greenvillian in ten has heard of this street, much less this church. Our deliveries and mail constantly end up at the more prosperous Northgate Baptist two blocks away. The other day the rabbi from the synagogue next door called me to say that he had just signed for a gallon of potato salad, three packages of rolls, and five frozen chickens that had been ordered for our congregational dinner; the delivery truck driver thought that Beth Israel looked more like a church than Northside.

Our congregation has begun a period of modest growth, but only after a great deal of effort in visitation. We have put up signs, taken out newspaper advertisements, and handed out maps in our attempt to help people find us. *"Where* is your church?'' visitors ask from a pay phone a few blocks away afer a Sunday-morning search for this elusive place.

In a way, I have always had trouble finding the church, Northside or any other. I have images of what a church ought to look like, not necessarily a building with a steeple, but a group of people who are committed, long-suffering, courageous in witness, and bonded together in love. I keep looking for that church. Every few years the bishop sends me to a new church. Things begin well enough; I think ''At last the bishop has sent me to a *real* church.'' Then, only a few months into that pastorate, I wake up to the harsh truth—the bishop has once again sent me to the wrong church. This church doesn't look like the real church at all. It is only a crude imitation, a sham. I keep looking and hoping. Where is the church?

I am not alone in my search. Hardly a week goes by without my meeting some dear person who cannot find the church, despite earnest efforts to do so. One of them first appeared at Northside during the hot August doldrums. A few months earlier he had moved to Greenville and, in his words, ''started shopping for a good church.'' I visited him at home and assured him that there was a good possibility that Northside was what he was looking for. We have a large number of young adult members, an active church school class for this age group, and a full program of projects and activities—to say nothing of the church's energetic, astute, caring pastor!

He visited for a number of weeks, attended the church school class, and came to one of our Wednesday night suppers. But his interest waned. After he had been absent for a couple of Sundays, I called on him to inquire if he had reached a decision.

''In the beginning I really liked your church,'' he said. ''I liked the worship services, and I enjoyed visiting in the church school classes. But frankly—I don't really mean this as criticism—the better I got to know your church people, the more I disliked them. You wouldn't believe some of the reactionary attitudes I heard expressed in the church school group. Also, I found your choir a bit disappointing on a couple of Sundays. No, I can't think of a lot of good reasons for joining a church that doesn't really grab me. I'm still looking for the right church. When it comes along, I'll know it."

Where is the church? More precisely, where is the *real* church, the *true* church? We are not the first to ask that question. "Where the bishop is, there is the church," said Cyprian. "Where correct doctrine is preached, there is the church," said some of the Reformers. "Where the visibly, consciously converted are gathered, there is the church," said the Anabaptists. Each of these is a partial image of the whole picture of where the church is to be found. We ask, "Where is the church?" out of our embarrassment that our church, the present church, never fully meets our expectations of what the church ought to be. We keep looking for something more.

In the Middle Ages this embarrassment led to the dualistic notion that there is (1) a "visible church," that is, the empirical human reality of the church as we see and experience it, and (2) the "invisible church," that is, the church as God intends it to be in divine perfection and fullness. No matter how bad things become in the church, one can always take heart that, even amid this disappointing assemblage, the true church is present, its identity and membership known only to God. The notion that there is some secret, invisible essence of the church within the present church appealed to the metaphysics of the day. It also reinforced the concept of the church as a repository of grace that transcends the limitations of actual people in actual churches at any given moment.

By stressing the invisible essence of the church, we admit to the essential incompleteness of any manifestation of the church. We are still pilgrims in our efforts to institutionally embody the love of God in Christ. We have not, nor have we ever, arrived. There is always something more. In a more positive sense, the visible-invisible metaphor affirms that the church is always something more than it appears to be. It is not another club or fraternal organization; the church is a chosen people, a holy nation. What appears to be a failing, decrepit, declining society of the religiously inclined is, in truth, none other than the very Body of Christ—though that holy Body may be invisible to the untrained human eye. The visible-invisible metaphor is an attempt, inadequate though it may be, to keep taut the tension between what the church is and what is called to be.

Generally speaking, the Reformers rejected the visible-invisible metaphor of the church. Calvin stressed that the essence of the church is its visibility, not its invisibility. That elusive "true church" that we seek is a visible society of the elect who are called by God to be the church. Talk of "visible" and "invisible" churches can be an evasion of the challenge to form a visible community of God here and now. Though Calvin would not reduce the church to a human institution alone, he does argue the commonsense observation that the church may be *more than* a visible society but it is not something *other than* that. Calvin therefore took issue with spiritualists like Schwenkfeld, for whom the church was only invisible—as spiritual individuals scattered over the earth.

The Augsburg Confession (Article VII) defines the church as "the assembly of all believers, in which the gospel is purely preached and the sacraments rightly administered according to the gospel." Though we may be bothered by the polemical tone of this definition and its (typically Lutheran) stress on correct belief as the chief identifying quality of the church, it does at least see the church as a visible and active assembly of people who come together in response to the gospel.

As one looks at the terms for the church in the New Testament, one is impressed by their concreteness, their visibility. The New Testament displays a luxuriance of ecclesiastical images; Paul Minear lists ninety-six different ways of speaking about the church.[1] The church is called saints (John 17:17–19), disciples (Matt. 28:19), believers and faithful (John 1:12), slaves

and servants (2 Cor. 4:5), people of God (2 Cor. 6:16), kingdom
and temple (Col. 4:11; Revelation 2–3), household and family
(Matt. 10:6), the new exodus (Hebrews), and the new humanity
(Rev. 14:4). This richness of New Testament ecclesiastical imag-
ery is indicative of the richness of this phenomenon we call the
church. The church is difficult to define, not because it is mysterious and invisible, but because it is seen and experienced in
so many guises. As Minear says, "The New Testament idea of
the church is not so much a technical doctrine as a gallery of
pictures."[2]

So to those who ask with dismay, "Where is the church?" our
best response is to point to that panorama of varied, visible
manifestations of the church and say, "*There* is the church."
The word *church* does not occur in the Gospels except for the
disputed passages—Matthew 16:18 and 18:17. The term is of
greatest importance in Acts and the Epistles. The Greek word
for church, *ekklesia*, means both the process of assembling together and the congregational assembly itself. The implication
is that the church is neither invisible nor a once-and-for-all,
fixed, and formed institution. It is a process.

The *ekklesia* is the visible result of a continuing process of
people coming together to worship God. We still talk about being "at church" rather than "in the church." Coming together
and staying together as the church is a never-finished process
for Christians. When the Lutherans said that the church happens in the assembly where "the gospel is purely preached and
the sacraments rightly administered," they were attempting to
avoid the medieval hypostatizing of the church—as an institution superior to formation by, and independent of judgment by,
God's Word. It keeps happening.

So the church is the church as an event of coming together, a
happening. We find the church not as an ideal, invisible, philo-
sophical abstraction but as a visible, specific gathering of people in the name and spirit of Christ. The real church is real people who can never be invisible. Therefore, I propose to find the

church by focusing on pictures of the real church: pictures of the church in the New Testament and pictures of the church as I have experienced it. I base my theology of the church, in great part, upon my experience of our church, because, for better or worse, this is the only church we have. We all wish the church would be more fully visible, more completely formed and available to us. Unfortunately, the world being what it is and we being who we are, we usually get only glimpses of the church as it ought to be. These brief manifestations in Scripture and experience disclose the larger reality of the church as it is called to be. I by no means put forth these particular pictures as ideal types or even models. They are pictures in a gallery that, when viewed together, complement one another, illuminating certain aspects of the church as a whole, but not all. They are testimony to the extravagance of God's ways with us.

No one congregation or biblical image embodies the whole church. My church needs other manifestations of the church to complement its expression of *ecclesia*. I think of it this way: A few years ago I spent a day in the Prado of Madrid viewing the paintings of Goya. His pictures ranged from light to dark, from formal court portraits to expressionistic, nightmarish sketches. "You are viewing the very soul of Spain," commented the museum catalog. And so I was. Here on the varied canvases of Goya was the face of a diverse, complex people. There were certain recurrent themes in the pictures. Some of the later pictures showed extremes of style or subject matter that, at first glance, seemed to come from the hand of another artist. And yet, upon closer examination, one could see that these pictures merely accentuated stylistic trends that had been present in Goya's art from the first. One needed to view all the pictures to appreciate the vitality and the richness of the artist and his country. However, this does not mean that if you have seen only one of Goya's paintings you have not seen a picture by Goya. In each painting you have indeed viewed "the very soul of Spain"—but not all of it.

The church is far richer than our individual experiences of it and more complex than any one New Testament ecclesial image. But this does not mean simply that the sum is greater than its parts. Your local congregation does not merely belong to the church; your local church *is* the church. It is not merely a cell of the larger organism but a manifestation of the whole organism. This suggests that the way to learn about the whole church is to look carefully at individual churches, all the while acknowledging that individual congregations do not exhaust the richness of the church universal. These congregations become rallying points for the universal church, centers for the never-ending process of congregating in the name of Jesus.

Extra Ecclesiam Nulla Salus

"He cannot have God for his Father who does not have the Church for his Mother," declared Cyprian.[3] No salvation outside the church—"*Extra ecclesiam nulla salus*"—has been the slogan through which the church attempted to counter those who attacked it. Vatican I (1869–70) responded to modernist detractors of the church by restating what the church had always claimed "Outside the Church no one can be saved.... Who is not in this ark will perish in the flood."[4]

Anyone with an even casual acquaintance with the average church may find the slogan "No salvation outside the church" to be a patent absurdity. We all know wonderful people outside the church—people even better than many within. For most of us, the church is an embarrassment. In Christian apologetics, the church is treated as something that must be explained or excused, a necessary evil at best, a hindrance to the advancement of the gospel at worst. I have heard television evangelists fulminate against the evils of "Churchianity" as opposed to "Christianity." And who can blame them? How far can one get urging people to come to Jesus with nothing better to commend this Savior than his would-be disciples in today's church?

In the American religious scene, one thing unites conservative and liberal Christians—their embarrassment about the church. American evangelicals are heirs to two formative movements of the last century that cast doubt upon the value of the church—pietism and revivalism. Pietism was in part a reaction to the arid rationalism of the eighteenth-century Enlightenment, in part a reaction against the divisive doctrinal disputes that had afflicted Protestants since the Reformation. Pietism, overreacting against the rationalism of the day, asserted the primacy of emotion in religion. Pietists like Philipp Jacob Spener (1635–1705) organized laity into small groups for Bible study, self-examination, and prayer. These *ecclesiola in ecclesia* ("little churches within the church") sought to renew the church through a committed laity. A personal, conscious, experiential conversion was said to be the only method of entrance to the Kingdom. Though pietism stressed the value of small groups, it tended to stress the individual's inner life even more, often at the expense of the individual's involvement in the church. Eventually many pietist groups that set out to renew the church became new churches (the Methodists and the Moravians, for example), but some pietists condemned any institutional expression of Christianity.

The other major influence on American evangelicals was the nineteenth-century revival. Revivalism proved to be an excellent means of reaching and converting the vast unchurched populace of early America. The revival shared pietism's stress on emotion as the source and test of true religion. Individual conversion was the goal of the frontier revival. The message of revivalist preachers was simple and straightforward—come to the altar and be saved. Revivalism tended to be more interested in winning converts than in nurturing or organizing converts. The sacraments were rarely mentioned by the revivalist, since disputes over sacraments and ordinances among American Baptists, Methodists, and Presbyterians were thought to do more to damage faith than to spread it. By the end of the nineteenth century, as revivalism became institutionalized in the citywide crusade under the leadership of men like Finney and Moody, churches were seen as a base for evangelistic effort rather than the purpose of the effort. Though revivalism accounted for the phenomenal growth of American Protestantism, it also formed Protestantism in this country into an expression of faith that tended to be apathetic toward the sociological realities of preserving and transferring Christianity from generation to generation. When the revival fires cooled, American churches sometimes found themselves cut off from the educational, liturgical, and theological structures that keep churches vital.

American Protestantism often impresses observers as a highly individualized, privatized, psychological affair, more interested in being successful or emotional than in being faithful. Individual conversion experiences—in which individuals are saved from individual sins in order to have individual relationships with Jesus—are viewed by some evangelicals as the end rather than the beginning of the life of faith. The church becomes a conglomerate of like-minded individuals who find it useful to congregate in order to keep the flame of individual religious experience alive and to foster it in others. About the best that can be said of the church from this viewpoint is that it is a necessary evil.

Although Protestant liberals distrust the church for somewhat different reasons than evangelicals, they are curiously like these conservatives in their stress upon faith as primarily a personal, individual experience. Kant and Schleriermacher set the tone for the liberals, in their stress upon the modern myth of the autonomous individual who obtains freedom by heroically extricating him- or herself from the past stories, groups, and shared values that society fosters. Religion is reduced to a matter of the emotions. The classical Christian expressions of faith are either scientifically explained away into irrelevance or psychologized into relevance. The individual's reason or emotion

is the supreme test of theological validity. Naturalistic reductionism and historical criticisms have taken their toll on the Bible, church history, and the experience of faith itself. In a de-
mystified world, there is little left for the church to do except to
be a sort of ethical society in which individuals are encouraged
to do something nice for others.

As a result of liberalism's attempt to relate the faith to the
modern worldview, churches that adopt the liberal stance toward the world are often scarcely distinguishable from the
world. Liberals distrust the church as an institution. It is
thought to be notoriously conserving and conservative by nature. Any group, including the church, threatens to erode
much-cherished individual autonomy. When the old evangelical fervor that fueled the Social Gospelers had dissipated, about
the best that liberals could say for the church was that it was a
potentially useful base of operations for changing society for
the better.

For the sake of brevity, I have discussed both the Protestant
evangelicals and the liberals as ideal types. Obviously, my sum-
mation does not do justice to all the points of view that may fall
under these headings. But I think it is accurate to say that, as
types, these two seemingly diverse perspectives have much in
common—particularly in their view of the church. They are
both children of the modern age and have assimilated well the
individualism, utilitarianism, and reductionism of the age.
They fit into an age of narcissistic self-gratification in their
stress upon the lone individual and his or her feelings and actions as the final test for everything.

One is hard-pressed to find many modern theologians who
have much good to say about the church. Most of the theologians who were influential upon my life fit this generalization.
The major exponents of neo-orthodoxy, from Brunner to Nygren, from Gogarten to Bultmann, were bored by liturgy, sacraments, pastoral care, and the concrete expressions of life in the
church. Those who sought to put Christian thought into exis-

tentialist categories were unashamedly individualistic and therefore suspicious of the church. Reinhold Niebuhr spoke of moral man—immoral society. Paul Tillich spent a lifetime addressing himself to Christianity's cultured despisers, especially the "latent church," as he called those good people who were not in the church. More recently, Karl Rahner has spoken of the "anonymous Christians"—those who do good without conscious or visible commitment to Christ. "No salvation outside the church" would have little appeal among these theologians.

In the 1960s, while I was in college and seminary, we were treated to a great number of books that pointed to the embarrassment of the church—as if this were something new. Gibson Winter's 1961 book, *The Suburban Captivity of the Churches*,[5] pilloried the churches as frightened enclaves of suburban bourgeois values. In the same year, Peter Berger's *The Noise of Solemn Assemblies*[6] forecast the death of the church as we had known it. About the best that Berger could say for the church was that it might serve as a caretaker for the more pitifully backward and helpless among us. The real mission of Christians was said to be in the world, not in the church. We were urged to "let the world set the agenda" and to use the church to change the world for the better. Many thought that the future of the church lay in shedding its institutional body, dismantling its network of agencies, dying, and coming forth like a butterfly from a cocoon, reborn as something fresh and new.

Such romantic reasoning about the church was a product of the established though patterns of the age rather than something radically new or anti-Establishment. Our age generally views institutional structures as inimical to individual human freedom. Little responsibility is felt for social continuity or multigenerational moral tradition. The struggle of our time is for individual autonomy (literally, self-law) against social repression. Great hope is pinned on the personal moral competence of the individual, who is expected to somehow single-handedly reconstruct the human situation better than any social tradition can. In other words, it is a time when the adolescent's struggle against oppressive parenting and against historical wisdom has become established in the worldview of the average American. Like the adolescent, we struggle to free ourselves from parental-like restraints and to chart our own course. This can be a necessary and healthy period in the developing adult's life; however, as most adolescents discover, the journey toward freedom is much more complex than we first believed it to be. Our freedom is won in great part through our ability to learn from our experiences, including our experience of history and our shared experiences within corporate structures. Ironically, the person who seeks to grow by loudly asserting independence from others, who seeks to keep all options open, never yoking him- or herself to social structures, stories, and a tradition finds that he or she only succeeds in falling deeper and ever more limitedly into the self. When liberation is defined as freedom from others, it becomes slavery to oneself.

The modern mind, contemptuous of premodern wisdom, absolutizing the values of autonomous individualism, caught in the adolescent refusal to be instructed by anyone outside the range of its own limited personal experience, naively optimistic about human progress, and trapped by narcissistic hedonism— no wonder it finds the claim of *"Extra ecclesiam nulla salus"* to be incomprehensible.

This fundamental distrust of the bodily, institutional, social quality of reality is not as new as it might appear. The romantic notion that truth can be discovered and circumscribed within the limits of one's own ego is not a particularly original concept; nor is the idea that the religious life can somehow be transmitted and sustained in ways that are other than social and institutional in character. Back in the 1950s Emil Brunner wrote *The Misunderstanding of the Church*, in which he contended that the original biblical *ecclesia* was something other than an institution. The church was a pure brotherhood, a divine rather than human substance, that had no place for law, sacraments, organization, and institutional apparatus.[7] Brunner thus presented the Body of Christ as something other than a visible, concrete, institutionalized body.

The church had heard this before. From very early times the church was tempted by the so-called docetic heresy, the belief that Jesus only *appeared* to be a man. (Docetism from the Greek *dokeio*, meaning "I seem" or "I appear"). Jesus was really a wholly divine being with only the external appearance of a human, the Docetists argued. Actually, Docetism was a tendency rather than a fully developed doctrine. Sometimes our tendencies, our unstated, unchallenged, undeveloped heresies, are the most dangerous. Docetism may have been a problem for the church even as early as the New Testament. The First Letter of John notes that "many false prophets have gone out into the world. By this you know the Spirit of God: every spirit which confesses that Jesus Christ has come in the flesh is of God" (4:1b–2).

The church maintained, against docetic tendencies, that Jesus was really present in the flesh, that he really did suffer and die with us. His body was a body like ours. His life was an earthly life like ours. Many who think of Christ in a docetic way believe that they thereby do him greater honor. By emphasizing Christ as something other than "in the flesh," they make him more holy, more divine. Unfortunately, the Docetists' subconscious motive is more likely to remove Christ to a safe distance. By making Christ into some disembodied, ethereal spirit, they render him irrelevant. Christ is not so disturbing or challenging as a being from outer space. We can sidestep the challenge of the Incarnation, because Christ only appeared to be for us, with us, beside us.

And if someone has docetic problems with the Incarnation, how much greater will be that person's problems with the church. He or she will admire Christ, find him attractive and inspiring, but will be repulsed by his Body. The idea of Christ is fine. The fleshly reality is repugnant. Like Brunner, the Docetist will argue that Jesus had something else in mind than the church when he called people to discipleship, something spiritual, pure, noncorporeal, not the church as we see it. By disembodying Christ from the church, the Docetist can be sure that Christ will not impinge on the facts of life. The suffering of Christ will be rendered only apparent, and his work will be kept hermetically sealed somewhere other than at 435 Summit Drive, Greenville, South Carolina.

In a romantic, docetic, anti-institutional milieu, the incarnational, bodily nature of Christian discipleship will be the chief scandal of the faith. People are fascinated by Jesus. But when they look at his poor Body, what do they see? C. S. Lewis's Devil describes the church visible as one of his best allies:

> One of our great allies at present is the Church itself. Do not misunderstand me. I do not mean the Church as we see her spread out through all time and space and rooted in eternity, terrible as an army with banners. That, I confess, is a spectacle which makes our boldest tempters uneasy. But fortunately it is quite invisible to these humans. All your patient sees is the half-finished, sham Gothic erection of the new building estate. When he goes inside, he sees the local grocer with rather an oily expression on his face bustling up to offer him one shiny little book containing a liturgy which neither of them understands, and one shabby little book containing corrupt texts of a number of religious lyrics, mostly bad, and in very small print. When he gets to his pew and looks round him he sees just that selection of his neighbours whom he has hitherto avoided. You want to lean pretty heavily on those neighbours. Make his mind flit to and fro between an expression like "the body of Christ" and the actual faces in the next pew.[8]

Few human beings become perturbed over what they cannot see; few risk their lives for invisible realities. It is the scandalous visibility of the church that bothers me.

Therefore, in thinking about the church, one must begin with the real church as it is rather than as we wish to God it were. This is an incarnational faith, not a disembodied abstraction.

Christians are called to exist in time and space, to be the Body of Christ here in our age and place. Only a visible church can be a home for human beings, a rallying point for this messianic movement that Jesus began. Today, more than ever, we must concern ourselves with the physical, visible church and search for ways that the church can be an even more visible and obvious statement of God's bodily presence in our world.

By its very existence, the church is an affirmation that one can never believe in God in the abstract. You can't believe in God without following God. Faith is not simply a matter of being attracted to certain beliefs or to a point of view. It is complete response, a way of life, a self-giving to someone else, a way of being in love. Christians are not those who are intellectually curious about Christ; nor are they those emotionally ravished and infatuated souls who have felt something stirring in their hearts. They are those who come forth to be disciples, to have their lives disciplined by the influence of the Master, to be yoked, to serve those whom he serves. The church is being in love, more like the love of a committed marriage than the love of a consuming but short-lived romantic attachment. There may be an "invisible religion" abroad in America, as Thomas Luckmann has noted,[8] a religion of those without social attachment or institutional expression. But Christianity is not it. This is not a home correspondence course in salvation. This religion is anything but a private affair. The New Testament depicts the Christian as one within a family, a household, a colony, a flock, a race, a body, a nation.

Now we are able to make more sense out of the church's astounding (to our modern ears) claim of *"Extra ecclesiam nulla salus."* This seemingly harsh and exclusionary doctrine is based both on actual human experience and on the nature of the Christian faith. It could be affirmed because people really did find salvation in the church; they discovered something there that they could not find alone. The doctrine was also a comfort to those poor worriers who were always taking their spiritual temperature and were always anxious about their salvation. To them the church said simply: "Relax, you are in the ark, safe from the flood. Your salvation is hereby taken out of your hands and placed in the hands of God and God's people."

"No salvation outside the church" is not a source of arrogance, or an encouragement for the complacency and moral condescension of the self-righteous. We are speaking of the norm for Christians, the normal means to come into and continue in this faith, the "ordinary means of grace," as John Wesley called the church. Our increased knowledge of cultural relativity warns us not to regard our particular church as absolute, as the one and only church. We have also experienced good, righteous, even Christian people who appear to be in the faith without being part of a church for some reason. However, the presence of these exceptions proves rather than disproves our norm of "No salvation outside the church." Because spiritual loners are such noteworthy exceptions, they confirm the church as the normal path for a Christian.

The church must take care in its attitude to those on the outside. I agree with Barth that the main difference between those who are in the church and those who are outside is noetic, a difference of those who know the fact of God's saving love and those who do not. The church is given responsibility for people outside the church; Jesus gives us the task of going into all the world to reach them. That baptismal mandate is laid upon the shoulders of the insiders rather than the outsiders. We are therefore not to judge those on the outside; we are only to testify as faithfully and humbly as we can to what has been revealed to us. The presence of large numbers of people who are apathetic or hostile to the church is an occasion for self-examination on the part of the church rather than aloof condemnation of the outsiders by the insiders. Our attitude should be like that of Paul toward his fellow Jews (Romans 3) rather than as Jews to Gentiles. Judgment always begins at home, with the chosen people whose chosenness carries with it the responsibility to be a "light to the nations."

And yet the fact remains: Salvation is not simply a one-time activity, a momentary event in an individual's life. The biblical picture of salvation is that of both an act of God and a state of being in a right relationship with God and one's neighbor. There is an arrogance and pharisaical self-righteousness among the churches and among the unchurched as well. We admit to the arrogance of some smug insiders who despise and ridicule the outsiders. But there is also the arrogance of those outsiders who feel morally and spiritually superior to those poor sinners in the church. As David H. C. Read has suggested,[10] today's new hypocrites may not be like the smug churchgoing Pharisee in Jesus' story who stood apart from the penitent publican and prayed aloud, "God, I thank thee that I am not like this sinful publican." Today's hypocrites are more likely to be those smug publicans *outside* the church who pray, "God, I may not be the best person in the world, but at least I am better than all those religious hypocrites in the church."

A pastor once told me about a man in his congregation who was very active in the life of the church but had never submitted to baptism. "Are you telling me that this man is unsaved because he has not been baptized?" the pastor asked.

We must separate two aspects of his question. If we are questioning whether God can save a person outside of the normal means of grace in the church, I suppose we could say that God is free to do anything, though finally this is a matter that is up to God, not us. But if we are questioning whether baptism is important for salvation from a human point of view, we must give an unqualified yes. I am not bothered by the man's misunderstanding about baptism. But I am bothered that the church has not proclaimed baptism, this evangelistic act of grace, in such a way that this man has come forward to receive it, and I am bothered by the man's implicit attitude that he is somehow either too good or too bad to be baptized. I am not as troubled by his attitude toward baptism as I am by his attitude toward the church. Baptism is an ecclesial, social sacrament, a sign that salvation is a group thing, a corporate gift of God working through the church to save us. To refuse that sign is to tragically misunderstand the working of grace in the church.

to Refuse baptism

It is no great achievement for people to reject the church today—we live in a hedonistic culture in the grip of "me-ism," rugged individualism, and the myth of the self-made man. Against this attitude, "No salvation outside the church" is an affirmation that God's grace is never appropriated in isolation. You do not hear this story or follow this way without help. The Christian life is too demanding, too tough, too at odds with our natural inclinations, to go it alone.

Many of those who criticize the church do so on the basis of an ideal. They set up a disembodied Platonic ideal, an abstract picture of the church, and then criticize the real church when it fails to resemble their fantasy. Of course, we must not simply take the status quo of the church as a standard and then attempt to justify that as the best the church can be. The church by its very nature is historical, social, and utterly human. It may be a "treasure in earthen vessels" (2 Corinthians), but it is the earthiness rather than the treasure that overwhelms us. Only by looking at the church realistically, that is, socially and historically, will we be able to see it for what it is.

Truth appears ambiguous to our eyes, because God's truth is communicated in mediated ways. Many saw Jesus but did not acclaim him as the Son of God. Even those who were earnestly looking for the Anointed One of God looked at him and asked, "Can any good thing come out of Nazareth?" (John 1:46). God is revealed through the obscure, the lowly, using the foolish, the weak, the low and despised to confound the wise and powerful. Is it any wonder that folk view this Body of Christ and wonder, "Can anything good come out of 435 Summit Drive?"

But the church's most severe and most accurate critics are always those on the inside rather than those on the outside. Others may criticize the church, but they are usually criticizing something they cannot understand, because they do not have the requisite faith commitment to make the church intelligible. The church can only be known, and therefore intelligently criticized, from the inside looking out.

As for those of us on the inside, we can do great damage to the church with our irresponsible, romantic speculations about the church. We do well to stick to the church as we have experienced it rather than setting up some ideal picture of a human community. Our romanticism and idealism can lead us to despair and cynicism when the church does not meet our ideals. Seminary shelves are full of books about the church written in the 1960s and 1970s that criticize the lethargy, the exclusiveness, the timidity, the conservatism, the defensiveness, and the boredom of the church. Really, now, what do these Docetists expect from so earthly, so human, an institution?

The zeal for the "underground church" and "basic communities" seems to have waned. The search for a perfect human community shed of institutional restraints is always illusory. One cannot sustain such hope for very long. We are humans, and our communities invariably reflect our humanity at its best and worst. As in Jesus' story of the wheat and the tares (Matt. 13:15–30), the final winnowing of the church into a purer and more perfect Body is not our job. Only God knows how such a division can be made and who shall be divided. The weeds and the wheat grow alongside one another until the Judgment. All attempts in the history of the church to bring about a premature separation of the good fish from the bad on the basis of human ideals have resulted in tragedy.

Dietrich Bonhoeffer's *Life Together* remains one of the most sublime visions of the church as a community. And yet, Bonhoeffer warns against our human penchant for idealizing the church and then evaluating and forming the church on the basis of our ideals.

Every human wish-dream that is injected into the Christian community is a hindrance to genuine community and must be banished if genuine community is to survive. He who loves his dream of a community more than the Christian community itself becomes a destroyer. . . . God hates visionary dreaming; it makes the dreamer proud and pretentious. The man who fashions a visionary ideal of community demands that it be realized by God, by others, and by himself. He enters the community of Christians with his demands, sets up his own law, and judges the brethren and God himself accordingly. . . . He acts as if he is a creator of the Christian community, as if his dream binds men together. When things do not go his way, he calls the effort a failure. When his ideal picture is destroyed, he sees the community going to smash. So he becomes, first an accuser of his brethren, then an accuser of God, and finally the despairing accuser of himself.[11]

The church is not *re*formed by idealists and romantics. It is *formed* by realists who know that commitment to Christ must be realistically, visibly embodied if it is to be faithful to the way of Christ himself.

Nor is the church reformed by simply redefining it in such a way that it loses its identity and embraces everything and everyone. Against theologians like Tillich or Rahner who speak of those "anonymous Christians" outside the church, "No salvation outside the church" protests against any ecclesiastical imperialism that would force everyone into the Kingdom by simply redefining the Kingdom without boundaries, form, or King. A Kingdom without boundaries, without distinction, is no Kingdom at all. How could Jesus have died for something so amorphous, all-encompassing, and vague? Talk about the "latent church" and "anonymous Christians" abandons the church as a historical, visible entity in its effort to make the church more palatable to an unbelieving world.

"No salvation outside the church" makes sense because of the biblical understanding that *salus* is not merely an opening of the gates of eternal life. Salvation is restoration, reconciliation, and healing, begun in the life and death of Jesus Christ and continued, however haltingly, in the church. Being "in Christ," as the New Testament sometimes says, means being in community with those whom Christ has called together. "No salvation outside the church" is not so much a judgmental declaration as it is an affirmation that, wonder of wonders, salvation does occur (even!) in the church.

As Barth says, for the church to stand and affirm with the Creed, "I believe in the Holy Catholic Church," is to say we believe that

at this place, in this assembly, the work of the Holy Spirit takes place. By that is not intended a deification of the creature; the Church is not the object of faith, we do not believe in the Church: but we do believe that in this congregation the work of the Holy Spirit becomes an event.[12]

The Quakers said that Jesus never intended to form the church. The church was an invention of his followers, a corruption of the primitive simplicity and purity of Jesus' message. But the scriptures show that Jesus' ministry was no impressionistic, momentary phenomenon. His ministry was directed toward the reconstitution of Israel. He came to inaugurate a new covenant and therefore a new covenant community. No first-century Jew would understand a messiah without a messianic community. Jesus is depicted as calling twelve disciples to correspond to the twelve tribes of Israel. Apart from Jesus' intention to form a community, the events of Acts are unintelligible. There, at Pentecost, the power of the Holy Spirit is given, not to individuals, but to the community. All who confessed Jesus Christ as risen Lord were banded together in a worshiping, serving, witnessing, and expecting fellowship. The nineteenth-century historian Alfred Loisy is often quoted as saying, "Jesus proclaimed the Kingdom of God, and what came was the church." But Loisy did not mean this in the cynical way in which it is often repeated, as if the church were a later misunderstanding of the original intentions of Jesus. Because Jesus proclaimed the inbreaking presence of a Kingdom, his presence and his message formed a distinct people.

We dare to affirm our commitment to the "Holy Catholic Church," not because we stupidly assume that the church is holy in the sense of pure, unspotted, unsoiled, virginal, and divine, we are using "holy" in the sense that the Bible uses the word. Again and again Israel is called a "holy nation," not because Israel is always faithful and pure—for that was certainly not the case—but because the nation of Israel was called into being by God for God's work. "For you are a people holy to the Lord your God; the Lord your God has chosen you to be a people for his own possession, out of all the peoples that are on the face of the earth" (Deut. 7:6).

Early Christians viewed themselves as the holy Israel of God for the same reason that Israel was holy: God had called this people for holy purposes. But you are a chosen race, a royal priesthood, a holy nation, God's own people, that you may declare the wonderful deeds of him who called you out of darkness into his marvelous light" (1 Pet. 2:9).

The Body of Christ

But the church's claim is even more dramatic—its claim is that it is one with Christ, bound in a relationship so intimate, so engaging, that only the most intimate of images can convey it. The church is "the bride of Christ" (Eph. 5:25–27; Revelation 21–22). The New Testament says that the church is Christ doing with the world what husbands and wives do with one another in marriage. This marriage is not fully consummated. The wedding has yet to be completed. The church has always to choose whether to be a faithful bride or a wayward harlot (Revelation 17 ff.). It is always a time of choice and struggle for the church, because the world can be seductive and the choice between love and lust is never easy. Yet this bride, for all her faults, is the one whom Christ has chosen. Now the church must forever choose Christ. The Old Testament frequently portrayed Israel as an adulteress. The church is no better. But the bride and Christ are so inextricably linked, by Christ's own action, that the church is more than just a finger pointing to God somewhere out there. The church is a visible sign of God's present love and fidelity right here.

Biblical images of the church become even more intimate. They say not only that the church is loved by Christ the way wives and husbands love, but the church is the very body of Christ himself. This incarnational faith asserts that "in the beginning was the Word, and the Word was with God, and the Word was God" (John 1:14). Jesus is God incarnate, "for in him the whole fulness of deity dwells bodily" (Col. 2:9). In saying that the Word was incarnate in Jesus Christ, we do not mean that God was somehow enclosed within the skin of this Nazarene. We mean that he was the center of the event of the Word becoming flesh. No human exists in isolation, but only in relation to other people. The Incarnate One includes the life, death, teaching, healing, and discipleship-producing acts of Jesus. The church, as the product of Jesus' ministry, is thus the extension of the Incarnation, his visible presence in Word and act, God among us.

From our struggle with the Docetists onward, Christian theologians part company with rationalist and idealist philosophers who try to reduce Christianity to a set of eternal truths. For this faith, the truth is a person—personal. "I am the way, the truth, the life" (John 14:6). Jesus represents the clash of the eternal with the temporal, the universal with the particular, the Word becoming flesh. To claim that the church is the Body of Christ is to say that the church participates in this same clash of the earthly and the heavenly. Its life is characterized by the same scandal that caused people to reject and crucify him. Embarrassment about the church as an institution is related to disease with a God who is incarnate.

How odd that Christianity should be periodically attacked for, of all things, enmity against the body. Nothing could be more fleshly, corporeal, and carnal than this faith. Who devalues the body—the church, or the world? those for whom bodily actions like coitus imply no commitment, or those for whom they necessitate irrevocable commitment? those who find recreation in casual nakedness, or those who reserve this mysterious revelation for those to whom they have something important to say? How ironic that the more our society detaches us from biological necessity and puts us at war with our own embodiment, the more that society is caught in frenzied pursuit of what it lacks. Christianity could be accused of having too high a regard for the body but not of despising it.

For the Christian faith, the church and its institution, sacraments, and rituals create a doorway into the world rather than an escape out of the world. The presence of some "pure" disembodied spirit would be slavery for us rather than freedom. Spiritualists and enthusiasts of every age who seek to soar from bodily realities end up trapped in the limited recesses of their own egos. At the spiritual summit, the air is rarified to the point of suffocation, and I am left with nothing to sustain me but myself.

The way the Bible tells it, God is never pure spirit. God is always embodiment, because this gracious deity has chosen to be available to his creatures, in dialogue. God's self-communication is always an address to me from outside in the form of a word spoken to me by someone else. It takes two to gospel: one to speak and one to turn around and pay attention.

So there can be no communion with God that is not also communion with one another. We do not look for God by gazing at idols, meditating upon ideals, wandering in the woods, or staring off into nowhere. We begin by looking at one another across the table. That's where we expect to "discern the body" (1 Cor. 11:29). So we speak about God's nearness by referring to such communal pastimes as meals, parties, bathing, processions, the kiss of peace.

Thus we can understand how Bonhoeffer could assert in *Life Together* that "Jesus Christ exists as Community." [13] A Platonist can celebrate the idea of Christ, a humanist can praise the ideals of Christ, but only within the Body of Christ can we know how the Christian can celebrate the very presence of Christ. The Body of Christ metaphor asserts, at the very least, that an individual apart from a congregation is a form of life that the New Testament does not envision.

Docetism cannot relieve us of the Christmas scandal. The Word has become flesh. Any separation of the spiritual and the sociological is not permitted. Like our own bodies, the Body of Christ is finite and limited. It cannot be all things to everyone nor do everything for the world. Institutions, no less than individuals, may long to throw off their bodies and rise up like Superman. But this childish wish is not to be. When people complain that the church is preoccupied with money, or closed-minded, or defensive, or lethargic, they are usually revealing their discomfort that the church is, indeed, a body. Bodies sweat, grow up, grow old, die, require maintenance. Some churches are the bodies of infants, stumbling, crawling, but full of promise. Some churches are adolescents, tripping over themselves, muscular, ready to take on the world, yet not always appreciating the difficulties of that task. Some churches are aged, declining bodies, bearers of proud memories and a distinguished heritage, but almost ready to keel over. For better or worse, in whatever body we encounter it, this is *Corpus Christi*, the form that our Lord has chosen to take in the world.

There are dangers in this sort of talk. For one thing, if we conceive of the church primarily as the Body of Christ, we might fall into making the church divine. Our union with Christ is not biological or hypostatic. One cannot attribute everything the church does to the presence of Christ in the church. The church is the creation of Christ, but it is not Christ.

However, this image does supply us with our basic answer to those who ask, "Where is the church?" The church is wherever

God calls it into being. The work of God, the call of God, makes the church the church. Its existence is not simply a sociological phenomenon; it is the result of God's incarnational self-giving, God's intercourse with the world. In the words of invitation to one of our modern creeds, "Where the Spirit of the Lord is, there is the one true Church."

The final scandal of the church, the ultimate stumbling block for us moderns, the real reason that we cannot locate it, is not so much that the church is human and therefore fallible and fallen but that the church is the peculiar creation of God that challenges our definitions of truth, holiness, salvation, justice, and goodness to their core.

The assertion "No salvation outside the church" is not a claim of exclusive prerogative or particular purity for the church; it is the faithful observation that salvation does not come to us by natural inclination, by birthright, or from within ourselves, and that the way of the cross goes against the grain or our notions of how the world is put together. Salvation comes from God alone, and therefore, it must be received on God's terms, not ours. Unfortunately for our illusions, God's terms require a way of life that is a social and an ecclesial gift. The hard truth is that we cannot find the church, not because it is invisible, but because, sinful as we are, we do not particularly like what we see.

2. Why the Church?

LIKE MANY people, I did not choose to be in the church, I was put there. Brought to church weeks after my birth, baptized when a few months old, I could say that it was the church who chose me. The continued presence and influence of the church over my life is proof that, contrary to American popular wisdom, the choices made for us and in spite of us are often of more lasting consequence than the choices made *by* us.

Life is full of choices. I like to think that my own heroic choices are the most determinative for my life. I enjoy thinking of myself as a Promethean chooser and shaper of my destiny. But in my better moments I must acknowledge that I have known God's grace principally through my experience that I did not choose God or God's church. The church chose me and thus reassured me that, in spite of my pretensions, salvation, mine or the world's, would not be entirely left up to me.

It was Main Street Church that first mediated this grace. Main Street exemplifies the Methodist penchant for naming churches for where they are rather than for some saint the congregation admires and for building churches that resemble a kind of holy First National Bank. There is neither steeple nor cross on Main Street. Its sandstone-colored stucco exterior, plain, neutral windows, and dignified Ionic columns might inspire an outsider to make a deposit there rather than say a prayer.

In the heart of downtown Greenville—two thousand members, some of the best-paid preachers in South Carolina, and a pipe organ manned by a belligerent organist who took pride in rattling windows and sending the "pillars of the church" fumbling to turn down the volume of their hearing aids—Main Street was big enough, complex enough, to overwhelm the doubts of a seven year old in a starched white shirt and itchy wool trousers.

I remember getting paid a silver dollar for memorizing the books of the New Testament. I remember Sunday school led by old Mr. Sanders, head of Primary Division, who told good stories of boys and girls who lived the way Jesus wanted them to—Mr. Sanders, who nearly always concluded the Sunday school assembly by leading us in a foot-stomping rendition of "We've a Story to Tell to the Nations," thus prompting the women's bible class on the floor below to send up an envoy to complain about the noise.

"Aren't these children wonderful!" Mr. Sanders would shout to the woman as we all marched and whooped,

> And the darkness shall turn to the dawning,
> And the dawning to noonday bright.
> And Christ's great Kingdom shall come on earth,
> The Kingdom of love and light![1]

Funny, but I can't remember much else about my earliest years at Main Street except long sermons and long prayers thanking God for "letting us be here today," which, to a boy of six or seven struggling to be still and quiet in the pew, seemed a dubious act of grace.

"Why do I have to go to church?" I remember asking my mother on many Sunday mornings, "I never get anything out of it."

Why indeed? When anyone asks, "Why the church?" whether at seven or seventy, it's a safe bet that he or she is really asking, "What's in it for me?" That is the chief concern of our age. What do we get out of this event called church?

I was in the fifth grade when I was put through a series of membership classes. I cannot remember anything done or said in those two months except an episode after the last class was over. I had missed the week before and had not heard Mrs. Jones's announcement that, at our last meeting, we would have our picture taken with the pastor for the church bulletin. Girls were to appear in party dresses; boys were to wear ties.

Upon my arrival at Main Street, I saw the harsh truth—everyone had on a tie but me. I decided to linger near the parking lot and intercept Dr. Herbert before he entered. There, I would offer to bow out of the picture gracefully, thus sparing myself the public humiliation of being asked to leave because I did not have the requisite neckwear.

"I didn't know that we were supposed to have ties," I haltingly confessed to the pastor.

"That's funny, because everybody else got the word," Mrs. Jones chimed in sarcastically.

"Well, well," said Dr. Herbert, "no tie. Now, I have on a tie because I'm the preacher here and I'm supposed to have one. But you aren't the preacher, are you?"

"No, sir."

"And I'm thinking," he continued, "but I can't recall anywhere in the Bible it says that you've got to have a tie to be in the church. Can you, Mrs. Jones?"

Mrs. Jones shook her head back and forth in silence, biting her lower lip.

"Well, if it's not in the Bible, then it must not be important. You go ahead and join us. We're glad to have you, tie or not," Dr. Herbert said with a wry smile.

Why the church? Because without the church, where does one learn that grace is always mediated? How does one hear or become a part of the Jesus story in isolation? That afternoon, standing in the back parking lot off Main Street, I got a glimpse of what the church was all about and what my baptism had got me into. Since that day, I've never been a proponent of rigorous confirmation classes and extensive membership training. Such artificial educational methods are of limited value for making

Christians. Most of us became part of the faith by simply watching our elders do it, by taking up a way of life, by imitating the actions and values of those whom we admire, by being put here by people like Dr. Herbert.

Originally, confirmation was a part of the baptismal rite that had to do with the church's confirmation of the new Christian. Typical of our individualized, near Pelagian approach to the faith, many today think of confirmation as a time for the growing Christian to confirm the church.

"Will you confirm our beliefs?" we ask. "Will you accept Jesus?"' we wonder. This gets the movement of faith backwards. Faith begins with God's confirmation, choice, and acceptance of us. I do not exist as a Christian save by the call of God. For that matter, neither did Israel exist as God's people except by God's choice. Likewise, the church is not church except that God wills it to be so.

There is something amiss in the definition of the church as a "voluntary association" of believers. The church does not exist because some religiously enlightened people have decided to voluntarily associate with one another to advance the study of Jesus. The challenge of biblical faith is not "Do you agree?" or "Do you feel?" but "Will you join up?"

Like Paul (Acts 9:1–31), like the Gentiles (Acts 15:14; Romans 9–11), like Israel, we are called together by God. "You did not choose me, I chose you" (John 15:16) is a word both humbling and comforting to the individual believer and to the church as a whole. The church begins, like faith itself, not with pious individuals, but with God, a God who chooses to deal with us as a people, a family, a nation.

Modern religion abhors organized religion. When a young woman told one of our church's visitation teams that she did not like "organized religion," a team member replied, "Well, you will be happy at Northside Church; we've been trying for thirty years but we ain't got it organized yet."

William James, pioneer of modern psychological society, described religion as a "white-hot heat" that burns for a moment in the solitary soul. Whenever one tries to extend this moment or embody it in some continuing, communal form, religion, James thought, has been compromised. I disagree. It is the social, political significance of religion that these modern individualists fail to grasp.

Why the church? is a question that may be answered sociologically before it is answered theologically. What do human beings get out of an institution like the church? We are asking the functional question, What does the church do for people?

A Colony of Heaven

Obviously, I believe the church is considerably more than another helpful human institution that serves some necessary human needs. And yet, though the church is more than this, it is not something other than this—as if these human needs were unimportant. The modern Docetist is embarrassed by the functional value of the church. Although sociological function is not the whole picture of the church, it is a significant part of the picture of an institution that is serious about people and their needs.

A few years ago, James M. Gustafson looked at the church as a human community in his *Treasure in Earthen Vessels*.[2] There, he reminded us that the church is not only a divine community, it is also a human, natural, political community. Earlier, Gustafson's mentor, H. Richard Niebuhr, had defined the purpose of the church and its ministry as "the Increase of the Love of God and Neighbor."[3] In other words, the church is the means through which we are encouraged to live the Great Commandment:

And one of the scribes came up and . . . asked him, "Which commandment is the first of all?" Jesus answered, "The first is, 'Hear, O Israel: The Lord of our God, the Lord is one; and you shall love the Lord your God with all your heart, and with all your soul, and with all your mind, and with all your strength.' The second is this, 'You shall love your neighbor as yourself.' There is no other commandment greater than these." (Mark 12:28–31)

This commandment is not only great in its nobility of sentiment but also great in its expectations for humanity. "Increase of the Love of God and Neighbor" is no small task. And so we have the church. In the church we gather the generations to recapitulate the story of God's dealing with us, to reaffirm our values, to name the Name, to identify one another as disciples. It is a place of refreshment and critique—in the world, but apart from the world.

Human beings are not transformed easily. We change not simply by coming to some different cognitive or emotional assessment of our situation but by entering into new relationships, entering into a new style of living in and viewing the world. "To have a conversion experience is nothing much," say two sociologists, "the real thing is to be able to keep on taking it seriously, to retain a sense of plausibility."[4] "Christians are made, not born," said Tertullian. In spite of what popular American evangelicism would have us believe, Christianity is not a momentary, instantaneous affair. It takes time, cultivation, work, perfection, reformation. The essential locus for that making of Christians is the crucible of the church.

Every congregation asks people to be more than mere consumers of religion, to discipline their instincts as private religionists and submit their faith to the scrutiny of the community. Outsiders are wrong in caricaturing the church as a kind of institutional crutch for weak faith. Instead, it is often the lone individual whose faith is so frail as to be incapable of surviving public testing. If Christians had not been called to change, to be converted, and then to continue to grow, the church would have lost one of its central functions.

We are creatures of habit, who do not self-sustain goodness, hope, and vision. Our values are both taught and caught from our social system. We may be socialized with the values of contemporary American narcissism, consumerism, materialism, and the host of other principalities and powers that surround us, or we may conform to a different set of standards. But be well assured that we will conform to some worldview or we will die. The question, therefore, is not whether we will fit into some society but which society will have its way with us.

My grandmother used to remark, when she heard that someone was ill, "They have been neglecting their habits." By this she meant that their lives had been chaotic and disordered, to the detriment of their well-being. Many today do not feel the presence of God, are not motivated toward any responsibility for their neighbor, sense no claim upon their lives, because they have been "neglecting their habits."

"I don't want to go to Sunday school today," declared our six year old.

"Why?" we asked.

"Because they never do anything new there," was his reply. "It's always, 'Jesus, Jesus, Jesus.' "

Ritual is a dirty word in our society. We value freedom, spontaneity, casualness. We write books that allegedly produce the joy of sex by advocating five hundred different positions in which to make love—pity the poor couple who does it the same way twice; this must be a sign that they are no longer in love.

Those who thus turn sex into recreation thereby ensure that our relationships will be kept on a superficial level. Most of us find that commitment requires a certain amount of sameness, repetition, and continuity; it takes time to grow, to deepen our understanding of ourselves and others. By reducing sex to a momentary, sporadic, brief encounter, one is protecting oneself from its threat and mystery.

Likewise, when religion is reduced to the momentary psychological high, the sporadic encounter, the two-Sundays-a-year drop-in, we are thereby protected from having this faith get under our skin, become second nature, a part of us. It will be only the brief happening, not the lifelong habit.

And so C. S. Lewis's Screwtape advises his apprentice devil

to keep his subject thinking that religion is a matter of high, momentary subjective flights of fancy and spirit rather than ordinary, daily outward habitual activity.

Keep his mind on the inner life. He thinks his conversion is something inside him and his attention is therefore chiefly turned at present to the states of his own mind. . . . Encourage this. Keep his mind off the most elementary duties by directing it to the most advanced and spiritual ones. Aggravate that most useful human characteristic, the horror and neglect of the obvious.[5]

The community of faith is characterized by ritual, sameness, repetition, by outward forms and old stories. Our claim is not that these stories and rites are original or exciting. Our claim is that they are true. Only by exposure to and surrender before this truth can one have the abundant life. In the church, the truth is constantly and habitually held before us until we either see or reject the truth.

Classical Christianity stresses not only that God in Christ pardons our sins but that God provides a community of forgiveness whereby we are enabled to actualize our freedom from the bondage of sin. To the Lutheran stress upon the justifying love of God must be added the Calvinistic and Wesleyan stress upon God's sanctifying love. The bare word of unconditional pardon would be immoral without a community concerned with the ever-deepening growth of the forgiven person. We are looking for the redemption not only of individuals but of society as well.

Thomas Oden uses this analogy: A governor pardons a criminal by signing an official act of pardon. But the act alone does not guarantee that the pardoned criminal will be motivated toward responsible behavior. Similarly, when Christianity declared that in the life and death of Jesus Christ our sin is pardoned it did so only from within the context of a faith community, which provided the structure for moral development through which the pardon might take form in the lives of those who knew the fact of their pardon. The claim that the cross makes a difference in people's lives is incomprehensible apart from a community of the cross.

Christian talk of forgiveness would be cheap if the recipients of it were not charged with actualizing that forgiveness in word and deed. On the other hand, the challenge to embody the love of God in Christ in our lives would be self-defeating were it not for the empowering love of a God that supports us through community. In later chapters we shall explore more fully the relationship of the church to the moral formation of Christians.

We are speaking of the church in a very mundane way at this point. We do so without embarrassment, for as we said earlier, we are participants in a most mundane sort of faith. It would be fine if we humans could make sense out of life *ex nihilo*, if we could honestly evaluate our lives on our own, if human growth could occur in a vacuum. From all that we know of human nature, people do not act that way—thus, the church.

Paul spoke of the church as "a colony of heaven" (Phil. 3:20). A colony is a beachhead, an island of one kingdom in the midst of another. The colony exists because, on their own, the individuals of the colony could never survive in the hostile environment of an alien empire. So they work and live together. The colony is not yet fully established, not out of danger. And yet, it is a haven of refuge, a beginning. In the colony, the stories, values, and customs of the homeland are carefully nurtured. The young are lovingly initiated into a way of life that the surrounding alien culture neither understands nor respects.

In my opinion, the American church does not adequately appreciate the precariousness of its existence within American culture. The world has stopped giving us favors. People will not become Christians by simply living within the country and watching television. We are aliens, exiles, colonists, more than we know.

In such circumstances, where Christianity returns to its status as a countercultural phenomenon, the functional, congregational, and institutional nature of the church becomes essential for the initiation, formation, and preservation of individual Christians. People will neither become nor remain Christians save through life in this colony.

And yet, in spite of all functional, mundane, sociological-psychological considerations, it is still true that the question, Why the church? eventually must confront the essentially non-utilitarian, scandalously nonfunctional nature of the church.

Sometimes people ask, "What difference would it make if there were no churches in your community?" Then they describe all the good things that churches do for a neighborhood. Or sometimes people try to justify the church as a means of social change or moral development. Under this line of reasoning, the church is simply a tool, a means to an end. This defense of the church has great appeal in a culture that asks of everything, "What good will it do me? Will it make me feel better? Will it work?"

Unfortunately, the church itself will not cooperate with its utilitarian defenders. A host of community agencies are more useful to the neighborhood. The church's record of changing individuals or neighborhoods for the better is notoriously mixed.

What is more troubling, the church has rarely claimed to do a great deal of good for people. If people become better while in the church, so much the better. But the fundamental claim of the church is that it, unlike some of its institutional competitors, forms itself around convictions and stories that are true. The only fundamentally sound reason for being a member of the church is that this is the only community that is consciously formed, criticized, and sustained by the truth. If a person does not believe, or is not at least on the way to believing, that this community is true, then that person's needs would be better served by joining a book club or Rotary. No matter how many good deeds and worthwhile contributions are credited to the church's account, if it cannot be said that the church is engaged in the business of responding to truth which is the person of

Jesus Christ (John 14:6), the church has no real point for being here, and its historic claims for itself are patently false.

The church cannot be defended as simply a useful means, a vehicle, for getting people a bit closer to God: It is a place of God. Wherever people are in the church, they have, in a great sense, fulfilled their existence. They are, at least partially, united with God. This divine-human union is its own reward. It is of intrinsic worth, regardless of whatever extrinsic good may come of it.

If I were to ask, "What good does being a friend of Mary Jones do you?" you might say to me that the question was out of place, inappropriate, a misunderstanding of the very nature of friendship. Undoubtedly, your relationship with Mary Jones influences your life in all sorts of ways. But none of that fundamentally describes why you are a friend of Mary Jones. Friendship has an intrinsic value, or else it is little more than manipulation, the cynical use of another person for your own selfish ends.

I think this is what the old Calvinists had in mind when, in the Westminster Catechism, they defined the "chief end of man" as "to glorify God and to enjoy him forever." You don't get any more "useless" than glorification and enjoyment; nor do you get any closer to the basic reason for the church.

There, in the parking lot of that fledgling colony of heaven that we called Main Street Church, I caught a glimpse of the glory of God. In one fleeting moment that has lasted a lifetime, the heavens opened, I saw God, and my frail life took on eternal significance. I sensed that I would make it, that it would not all be left up to me, that my name had been called, that there was a kind of graciousness lifting me up. In short, I came to worship. I lifted up my shoulders and glorified and enjoyed God with all the gifts that I had received in ten years of life.

I can't tell you what "good" that episode with Dr. Herbert did me. But somehow, even for one as young as I, I knew that it was a kind of irrefutable answer to my "Why do I have to go to church?"

Who Makes the Church?

In the final analysis, the question, Why the church? can be answered only by reference to the work and purposes of God, because God, for reasons that may appear unreasonable to us, wants the church. Why am I a Christian? because God chose to deal with me in this peculiar way—through parking lot revelation and all the other means whereby God put me where I am today.

The Bible is clear that, in relations between God and humanity, the initiative always lies with God. The Creation is the object of God's never-ending care and concern. The church is simply one more example of God's extravagant, creative involvement with his world. Why here and not elsewhere? I do not know. We can only testify to what we have seen and heard and touched, even though we cannot explain: God wants the church.

There is a word of grace here for us pastors. From time to time we get the erroneous impression that God wants us to be builders of the church rather than custodians of what God builds. So we work long hours—visit, plan, preach—because, if we don't make the church, who will?

In our better moments we know better. The church exists because God wills it to be. The church has always had too much going against it, too many negative forces, too many reasons why it should not be here at all, for its continued presence in the world to be explained in any other way than as an act of a gracious God who wills that we should not be left alone, that it should not all be left up to us.

The most important fact about the church is, therefore, the presence of a Savior who calls people to himself, sustains them by his grace, and works through them to carry out his mission. Among Protestant and Roman Catholic scholars, there is consensus today that the most important thing about the church is its existence as the result of the divine self-giving in Christ. *Ubi Christus, ibi ecclesia*, was the Latin tag that once expressed this truth: Where Christ is, there is the church.

The church is a post-Easter phenomenon. It was the astounding, unexpected presence of the risen Christ that formed a believing community. Without that presence, the church might have been described as a memorial society or a reunion for old veterans of the Jesus campaign, laboring to keep alive the fading memory of a dead hero. When the New Testament speaks of the "church of Christ" (Rom. 16:16), it does not mean that the church traces its origins to any particular command of Jesus', or to his teachings, or to his organizational ability. It is his personal presence as the risen Lord that originates this colony that we call the church. The account of the birth of the church in Acts 2 depicts this movement from recognition of presence to formation of the community. The Jews believed that the Spirit had deserted Israel after the time of the last prophets. The Spirit's presence was promised again during the last days and would be evident in a variety of ways: new prophets, acts of power, finding the right words when on trial before the governing authorities. At Pentecost, in the descent and presence of the Spirit, that New Age is now.

Jesus is not important to the church primarily as a great moral teacher or an inspiring philosopher. His present life is the vitalizing center of the people. That is why we speak of the "real presence" at our celebrations of the Lord's Supper. This family meal is our witness that the crucified and resurrected Lord is present, not as a projection of faith, but as that fact to which the family's faith is the appropriate response.

When we look at the church and our experience of its institutional variety or look at its checkered history, we may ask what on earth unites this disjointed story. The answer is: the presence of the risen Christ in the midst of the community. No part of the church's history, within the complex of two millennia of Christian languages, cultures, and worldviews, is without some form of encounter with the risen Christ. "I am with you always," says Jesus to his disciples, "to the end of time" (Matt. 28:20).

No matter how our major theologians differ, no matter how they express their perspectives on Christian truth, they do not differ in their affirmation of the center of that truth: Christ is present in the church in the past and even now, in spite of the most drastic historical reversals and cultural changes. The person who is able to say, "The life I now live is not my life, but the life which Christ lives in me; and my present bodily life is lived by faith in the Son of God, who loved me and gave himself up for me" (Gal. 2:20) is the person who is close to the center of the church's life. "Did we not feel our hearts on fire as he talked with us on the road and explained the scriptures to us?" (Luke 24:32) is the experience of worship that calls the church into being and gives it vitality. Christianity is nothing more nor less than participation in the believing community of Jesus' death and resurrection.

"Why do you stand gazing up into heaven?" the disciples were asked once the risen Christ disappeared from their sight (Acts 1:11). The church is not to remain dumbly staring off into space, because the Resurrection is not its end but its beginning. The once disheartened disciples, so impressed with their own finitude, stupidity, infidelity, and smallness, became the Body and, in so doing, turned the world upside down. The ultimate proof of the Resurrection is not an empty tomb or the Shroud of Turin. The ultimate evidence for the Resurrection is the existence of something so unlikely and inexplicable as the church. One cannot explain the birth or the impact of the church in any other way except as the resurrected Body of Christ.

It is never easy to come together or to stay together in the church. It is not easy because Christ called to him such diverse and dissimilar people. It would be well nigh impossible to have unity in the church were it not that our unity is the result, not of good-hearted feelings of fellowship for one another, but of the reality created by the presence of the risen Christ in the midst of his people. The New Testament speaks of this Christocentric unity by calling Christ the Vine and church members the branches (John 15); Christ is the Shepherd, we are the sheep (John 10); he is the head of his Body, the church, of which we are organic members (1 Cor. 12:12–27; Eph. 4:11–16). "For as in one body we have many members, and all members do not have the same function, so we, though many, are one body in Christ, and individually members one of another." (Rom. 12:3–5).

The unity he creates is not for a cozy mutual admiration society. The source of our unity is also the impetus for our mission. The whole vine grows; there are yet "other sheep" who must be brought in; the Body is edified and grows until the "fullness of Christ" is attained in the time of the completion of his Kingdom.

Once we see the presence of Christ as the center of the church, everything the church does makes more sense. The church's experience of human encounter is seen as a fruit of the divine-human encounter. We are able to love others, even those who do not love us, because we have been loved. Our participation in the day-to-day mundane life of the church is seen as *participatio Christi*. Pastoral care becomes sharing in the work of Christ. Preaching becomes participation in the proclamation of Christ's presence in daily life. Worship is experienced as an enactment of the bodily presence of Christ. Our ethics is the sharing of God's loving activity in the world. In later chapters of this book, we shall explore these activities as the church's living out of its experience of the living Christ among his cherished people.

Because Christ (rather than our efforts or ideals) is at the center of the church, the church must always be open to new and ever-greater exploration. Because God is great, mysterious, and ever surprising, the church must be adventurous and open to surprises in its continuing dialogue with its Lord. It must never cease to reflect upon the source of its life. That is why the church is *ecclesia semper reformanda*. We are always en route, our eyes always looking for that new city that God is building among us (Hebrews 11).

Reflection on the real life of the church in its concrete, congregational manifestations would be unbearably discouraging were it not that our hope is not in ourselves and our ability to be the church but in Christ and his ability to create what he desires. When the New Testament speaks of "the church of God," it reminds us that the church exists because God wills it (Acts 20:28; 1 Cor. 1:2). "You didn't choose me, I chose you," is not only a statement of fact about our origins but also a source of comfort for our struggles. This Body was not our idea, so we need not sustain the church on our own. It is God's gracious creation, not our achievement. When Angelo Roncalli assumed the great burden of the church as Pope John XXIII, he comforted himself at night with this prayer: "But who governs the church? You or the Holy Spirit? Very well then, go to sleep, Angelo."[7]

The gifted nature of the church enables those of us in the church to take heart even amid so many disheartening circumstances. Bonhoeffer says that the church

is a gift of God which we cannot claim. Only God knows the real state of our fellowship, of our sanctification. What may appear weak and trifling to us may be great and glorious to God. Just as the Christian should not be constantly feeling his spiritual pulse, so, too, the Christian community has not been given to us by God for us to be constantly taking its temperature. The more thankfully we daily receive what is given to us, the more surely and steadily will fellowship increase and grow from day to day as God pleases.[8]

We are the thankful recipients rather than the creators of the church; therefore, we can relax and enjoy what grace the church is able to receive and embody.

The church is justified by faith no less than are individuals. Thank God.

3. In, But Not of, the World

CENTRAL CHURCH, New Haven, was a long way from Main Street Church, Greenville—as far as Yankee Connecticut is from the Old South. When I went to New Haven as a student at Yale Divinity School in 1968, I felt as if I were fortunate to be escaping the South. The civil rights movement had bogged down. Vietnam protests were getting ugly. It was a privilege to leave the backward, benighted South for the intellectually sophisticated, progressive Northeast.

Central Church represented everything that I admired then—an intellectual congregation, two erudite pastors (including a young one who smoked a pipe, had long hair, and made biting comments about the Establishment), and a generous endowment. We attended Central Church on Sundays, where we were treated to one of the best string ensembles in town (they played a piece at the beginning of the service and then packed up their instruments and left—their contract did not include staying to worship).

The ministers delighted in shocking the congregation with "innovative worship"—balloons one Sunday imprinted with the words To Hell with Nixon-Agnew, a jazz combo the next. It should be noted that there were not many people to shock on a Sunday morning at Central Church. The eighteenth-century meetinghouse that was designed to accommodate five hundred worshipers overwhelmed the fifty or sixty who now attended Central. The low attendance bothered me, so I asked one of the pastors about it.

"Of course, you are from the South, the Bible Belt, where religion is still 'in,' " he said to me condescendingly. "Here in New England, all that is past. Only the fundamentalists attract many people. And we all know the reason for that."

I wasn't sure of the reason, but I wasn't about to let him know.

"Besides, since we have made Central Church politically active" (the "we" here meaning the two pastors) "some of the dead wood, the backward types, little old ladies and such, have been weeded out."

His implication was that no one came to Central anymore except the politically enlightened and the socially sensitive. In reality, Central Church had been reduced to a pitiful huddle of people, most of whom doggedly kept coming "because my family has always been a member of this church" or because, like me at the time, it was a way to go to church without really going to church.

Eventually, Central Church hired my wife and me to teach in the church school. As students, we desperately needed the money, so we were delighted when the job was offered. Central had a tradition of hiring people to teach. They were proud of having a church school run by "professionals." In fact, Central hired "professionals" to do nearly everything that was done around the church, from the janitorial work to the music, because no one else would do it. For fifteen dollars a Sunday, we taught a total of ten or twelve children. We were asked to use no curriculum but, rather, to "let the children express their feelings about religion" and "explore themselves." Translated into plain English, this usually meant watching the children run wild in the fellowship hall for an hour, although one time we had a talk by a Buddhist monk who was working on a sociology degree at Yale. The Buddhist's lecture was about the only religion I remember exposing the children to during my time at Central Church. It was years later before I read Peter DeVries's wicked satire on the modern church, *The Mackerel Plaza*, in which he describes "People's Liberal Church":

Our church is, I believe, the first split-level church in America. It has five rooms and two baths downstairs—dining area, kitchen and three parlors for committee and group meetings—with a crawl space behind the furnace ending in the hillside into which the structure is built. Upstairs is one huge all-purpose interior, divisible into different-sized components by means of sliding walls and convertible into an auditorium for putting on plays, a gymnasium for athletics, and a ballroom for dances. There is a small worship area at one end. This has a platform cantilevered on both sides, with a free-form pulpit designed by Noguchi. It consists of a slab of marble set on four legs of four delicately differing fruitwoods, to symbolize the four Gospels, and their failure to harmonize. Behind it dangles a large multi-colored mobile, its interdenominational parts swaying, as one might fancy, in perpetual reminder of the Pauline stricture against those "blown by every wind of doctrine." In back of this building is a newly erected clinic, with medical and neuropsychiatric wings, both indefinitely expandable. Thus People's Liberal is a church designed to meet the needs of today, and to serve the whole man. This includes the worship of God free of outmoded theological definitions and palatable to a mind come of age in the era of Relativity.[1]

DeVries must have had Central Church as his model.

"Social concern" at Central meant pet projects of the pastors: they got the church board to agree to send checks to suitably controversial groups, and then bragged about it at clergy meetings. They once gave ten thousand dollars to the Black Panther Defense Fund in New Haven and were most disappointed when no one in town complained.

"I expect there's not another church in America that could get away with some of the activist things we do," commented the senior pastor one Sunday. True. Few churches in America have a three-million-dollar endowment or congregants who couldn't care less what is done in the name of the church.

By the time I was ready to graduate, I had had enough of Central Church. I had ceased to be even amused by the program of social activism at Central—after you have been host to the first regional conference on lesbian rights, what else is left for a progressive church to do? Now I was mostly bored. All the talk by the pastors about "tightening our ranks for service" and how unusually liberal and open the folks were at Central turned out to be a convoluted way of saying that Central was dying. I gave the church ten more years before it would be a congregation of two avant-garde pastors, ten aging New England aristocrats—and their three-million-dollar endowment.

"You must remember that you're from the South, which is at least a decade behind the Northeast, intellectually speaking," said the senior pastor to me a week before I was to graduate from seminary and head home. I told him about my discomfort with Central Church and its program. "We are where the liberal, progressive churches of your area will be ten years from now," he predicted, with just a hint of defensiveness in his voice. "Our church is involved in the major issues of the day," he said. "We're getting out of our cloisters and into the streets. That's where the action is."

The last sermon I heard at Central Church was a book review of *The Greening of America.*

Central Church illustrates the dilemma of the church in the world. In the world, a little salt goes a long way. But how does one keep the church's salt from losing its savor? Beginning in the 1960s, there was much talk about the social activism of the churches, the need for the church to be "in the world." Many mainline Protestants found themselves engaged in a variety of political activities—all in the name of Christ. Churches played no small part in the civil rights movement, the antiwar movement of the 1960s and early 1970s, and the antinuclear movement of the 1980s. We Christians sought to be the leaven of the world.

But leavening and enlightening the world are no small tasks. Time and again in our history, the church has been dismayed to find that, in setting out to convert the world, the world has often subverted us. Social concern is a legitimate Christian vocation. But what kind of concern, and to what end? In this book we have put forth a view of the church as a social, political, and institutional fact. The question is never, "Should Christians be involved in the world?" We already are involved in the world—we live, vote, eat, sleep, and buy and sell in the world. Our Lord calls us not to form a cozy little club of the religiously inclined but to help him turn the world on its head. We cannot be who we are as the church without being involved in the world.

But what is our proper involvement? What is the church's proper stance toward the world that surrounds us? These are major questions for the next decades, questions that this chapter attempts to answer by using Central Church as a catalyst to our thinking about the church in the world.

How in the World?

From what I observe, when the world looks at the church today, particularly the American world looking at the American church, the world is not trembling in its boots because the church is getting too big for its breeches. More than likely, what the world sees in the American church is not a people who are converting the world but another organization that is trying to preserve peace in the world. Our leaven is weak, and our salt has lost its savor. Will Campbell, that great Southern Baptist prophet, was confronted by one of his friends, who called the church a mere "Easter chicken" in its relationship to the world:

"You know, Preacher Will, that Church of yours and Mr. Jesus is like an Easter chicken my little Karen got one time. Man, it was a pretty thing. Dyed a deep purple. Bought it at the grocery store."

I interrupted that white was the liturgical color for Easter but he ignored me. "And it served a real useful purpose. Karen loved it. It made her happy. And that made me and her Mamma happy. Okay?"

I said, "Okay."

"But pretty soon that baby chicken started feathering out. You know, sprouting little pin feathers. Wings and tail and all that. And you know what? Them new feathers weren't purple. No sirree bob, that damn chicken wasn't really purple at all. That damn chicken was a Rhode Island Red. And when all them little red feathers started growing out from under that purple it was one hell of a sight. All of a sudden Karen couldn't stand that chicken anymore."

"I think I see what you're driving at, P.D."

"No, hell no, Preacher Will. You don't understand any such thing for I haven't got to my point yet."

"Okay. I'm sorry. Rave on."

"Well, we took that half-purple and half-red thing out to her Grandma's house and threw it in the chicken yard with all the other chickens. It was still different, you understand. That little chicken. And the other chickens knew it was different. And they resisted it like hell. Pecked it, chased it all over the yard. Wouldn't have anything to do with it. Wouldn't even let it get on the roost with them. And that little chicken knew it was different too. It didn't bother any of the others. Wouldn't fight back or anything. Just stayed by itself. Really suffered too. But little by little, day by day, that chicken came around. Pretty soon, even before all the purple grew off it, while it was just a little bit different, that damn thing was behaving just about like the rest of them chickens. Man, it would fight back, peck the hell out of the ones littler than it was, knock them down to catch a bug if it got to it in time. Yes sirree bob, the chicken world turned that Easter chicken around. And now you can't tell one chicken from another. They're all just alike. The Easter chicken is just one more chicken. There ain't a damn thing different about it."

I knew he wanted to argue and I didn't want to disappoint him.

"Well, P.D., the Easter chicken is still useful. It lays eggs, doesn't it?"

It was what he wanted me to say. "Yea, Preacher Will. It lays eggs. But they all lay eggs. Who needs an Easter chicken for that? And the Rotary Club serves coffee. And the 4-H Club says prayers. The Red Cross takes up offerings for hurricane victims. Mental Health does counseling, and the Boy Scouts have youth programs."[2]

In his book *Righteous Empire*, Martin Marty divided American Protestants into two opposing parties: the public Protestants and the private Protestants, one characterized by liberal this-worldliness, the other characterized by conservative otherworldliness. All of American Protestantism, Marty argues, could be divided and explained in terms of these two polarities.

Many of us wonder if Marty's neat distinction has now collapsed. First came the New Evangelicals, the Jim Wallises of Sojourners applying conservative, evangelical theology to public concerns: peace, hunger, military buildup, economic justice for women and minorities. It was good for us liberal social activists to welcome these Johnny-come-latelies into the fold.

But then came a new force. The 1980 election threw Pat Robertson, Jerry Falwell, the Moral Majority, and Christian Voice into the public arena. What were their concerns? Peace, hunger, economic justice, military buildup, women, minorities. We were confused.

Then there was Jimmy Carter mixing certified liberal causes with down-home Southern Baptism private pieties. Confused liberals deserted Carter and sat out the 1980 election. Nobody was playing by the old rules.

"Foul," cried the former public Protestants—former public Protestants who now, more than likely, were out of the political arena (where the fight had become dirty, indeed) and into spirituality, autobiographical theology, or other very private concerns. Liberal cries of outrage against the rise of the Moral Majority sounded a bit hollow. After all, the New Right was only doing what the Old Left once did: pushing a social and political agenda on the body politic in the name of Jesus, transposing the claims of Christ into public policy.

Earnest efforts on the part of us Old Lefters to distinguish our tactics for sociopolitical involvement from those of the New Righters have been unconvincing.

I believe that we're seeing more than a breakdown of the public-private typology—we're in a crisis that requires rethinking of the whole relationship of the church to national politics and public affairs. It is time for a complete reappraisal of how mainline Protestants relate to American life.

At least since the social crusades of the early nineteenth century, there has been a sort of consensus that mainline Protestant churches had the obligation to "go public" with their program and work through sociopolitical structures to change American society for the better. But suddenly we have two competing, colliding social programs being pushed by Christians. Would the real Christian political program please stand up?[3]

Nobody I know seriously questions whether Christians ought to be involved in the world. As I said earlier, we are already "in the world," like it or not. We vote, buy, sell, eat in the world; our religious actions and beliefs have sociopolitical consequences and vice versa. For another thing, Jesus Christ is Lord, Lord of nations no less than of churches and individuals. He must reign until he has put all things under his feet.

So the question is not *whether* we shall be involved or concerned politically, but *how*.

In a more recent book, *The Public Church*, Martin Marty still uses the public-private typology, all evidence (i.e., the Moral Majority) to the contrary. But Marty now notes that many of us mainline denominations have had more success relating to the public order than being the church.

As Marty says, in being open to involvement in the *res publica*, we haven't been "discriminatingly open." In our concern to use political activism to put the national house in order, many of us mainline Protestants have failed to take care of business at home.

Recently, one of our church boards was drafting a resolution to our state legislature requesting the expenditure of more funds to aid handicapped people. A handicapped woman spoke out. "You hypocrites. I doubt there is a person here from a church that is totally accessible to the handicapped. How many of you have Sunday school classes for the retarded or a transportation committee for your elderly shut-ins?"

Her words hit home. It is always easier to dictate morality from the safe anonymity of public policy, to spend someone else's tax money, to advocate that the state work justice rather than doing justice in the church. The social activism of most liberal, mainline denominations sound as if someone has asked us Christians to run the government rather than be the church. In so doing, we are unrealistic about our effect upon both the present political situation and the unsuspecting victims of an inadequate ecclesiology.

If I remember church history correctly, the persistent problem is not how to keep the church from withdrawing from the world but how to keep the world from subverting the church. In each age, the church succumbs to the Constantinian notion that we can get a handle on the way the world is run, take charge, fit the world's standards of justice into a loosely Christian framework, substitute a little worldly wisdom for gospel foolishness, talk power rather than love, and call this "Christian social concern." Whenever the church has sought to prop itself up by the power of Caesar or the democratic mob, trusting the power of legalistic coercion rather than trusting the power of truth, the world has successfully co-opted the church. Today, liberation theology, having decided in whose hands lies the political future, tells the church to exchange capitalist bedfellows for Marxist ones. Then, when the revolution is over, the church will get to help run the world. Today, the Moral Majority declares that this is a Christian country and legislatively tries to force everyone to accept the moral standards the Moral Majority cannot achieve even in their own churches. Long before the Religious Right, we liberals decided that "social concern" meant the politics of power rather than the witness of the cross. We began improving the world rather than reforming the church. As a result, we have what the theologian Moltmann calls a "chameleon theology" in which an acculturated church, baffled by its inability to have an impact on society, merely blended into society, became the victim of every passing fad, and politely waited, hat in hand, for something useful to do to help keep society intact.[4] So our pastors are now referred to as "helping professionals," and the President urges churches to make themselves useful by taking up the slack in welfare programs.

Thoughtless social involvement and indiscriminate openness have led to a crisis of identity. As I see it, our mainline Protestant problem is not that we are out of the world, but that we are not there on our own terms. I do not share Martin Marty's optimism for the "public church." As Lyle Schaller said of my United Methodist Church during a speech in 1983, having talked so much recently about the need for the church to "serve the community," now we need to reflect upon how to build a community in the church.

You misread me if you hear in this a retreat from social concern, a new narcissism for the church. I am pleading for a more radical concern, an engagement with American society on our own terms, a social activism that is appropriate for those under the cross who constantly wonder what it means to "not be conformed to this world" (Rom. 12:2), those who recognize Jesus Christ as Lord.

A church that expends too much energy leaning over to speak to the world sometimes falls in. When it comes to social problems, the strategies of most mainline, liberal denominations imply the anachronistic assumption that it is up to government to do right or right will not be done. Rather than criticize, they mirror the contemporary American preoccupation with competing rights and privileges and narcissistic self-affirmation. We show a curious split between private and public morality. Stanley Hauerwas has criticized the liberal church for being "public legalists and private antinomians."[5] We couple a laissez-faire attitude toward personal morality with a legalistic, coercive stance on public policy, confidently asserting what ought to be done on all sorts of complex global problems but utterly confused about what to say to two people in a bedroom.

Recently, a woman in my church asked me, "What does our church believe about divorce?" It was a logical thing for her to ask. She was contemplating a divorce and rightly sought guidance from her church on the subject. I gave her the paragraphs from the *United Methodist Social Principles* to read.

"About all I can tell is that we believe that divorce is not a good thing to do, but in some cases, it is a good thing to do," she said after reading the paragraphs. "Our church seems to think that the main thing is to do what you personally think is right. What help is that?"

The ethical assumptions that underlie such liberal morality are the ideology of democratic, egalitarian capitalism rather than the peculiar story of the people of God. It doesn't require a great amount of courage for a church to say to contemporary American culture: First be sure in your heart that what you are doing is right, then go ahead and do it and to hell with what anybody else says.

The world must think that our social pronouncements are rather tame, because we have universalized and generalized our principles in hopes of making them applicable to American society as a whole rather than to the people of God in particular. In approaching ethical problems, we cannot afford to refer to the biblical witness, or even church tradition, because we are attempting to reduce our stance to a position every thinking, sensitive American can affirm. Everything must be yes and no because we cannot speak of sin to those who do not know a standard of justice other than their own opinion, who do not know a God who forgives.

A church that no longer preaches grace cannot afford to admit the presence of sin in every human activity, even the most rational and most sensitive. All it can do is to moralize, tell people to do the best they can, and preach sincerity as the sole ethical criterion. We dare not aspire too high in our ethics when speaking to a people who think that they are the sole fabricators of what is good. We cannot be too critical of conventional American ethical wisdom when our goal is adaptation to the world rather than conversion of the world.

And so we present Christian morality as something that

makes good sense, something that will help keep American society running smoothly, something that will aid in our national survival. We thus imply that it is possible to live the Christian life without holding the Christian faith. Any thinking person should be able to affirm the Ten Commandments, the Sermon on the Mount, Paul's ethical injunctions, we say. We thus fail to do justice to the radical quality of Christian ethics, which are based more on affection and obedience than reason and practicality. We jettison the faith commitments that make distinctively Christian ethics intelligible. This leaves us with a social concern with little more to back it up than sentiment, open-mindedness, pragmatism, and expediency.

All of this is to say that the church's particular way of relating to the world must arise out of who the church is. In earlier chapters of this book we have sketched a view of the church that placed the church *against* the world in order to be truly *for* the world. We spoke of the church as a countercultural phenomenon, a colony of heaven. Whatever we say about the church's social concern must arise out of this view of the church. My criticism of mainline, liberal Protestantism (such as I first experienced at Central Church) is that its churches are unable to be very critical of the current social order, since they rely upon this order as a prop for a church more concerned with being attuned to the status quo than being truthful. In our approach to social problems, we have decided to be honey to help the world's solutions go down easier rather than the salt of the earth. We have trusted governmental legislative coercion rather than the power of our witness to the truth. In so doing we have given the world evidence that truth alone is not strong enough to preserve the church.

Taking Care of Business at Home

The crucial political, social-activist question for the church is, *What kind of community do we need to be in order to be faithful to*

Christian convictions? The church always exists in congregation, a congregating of those who have been called forth to live the truth which is Jesus Christ. That coming together is the dynamic that is at the heart of the church as a political event. Our primary task is not to give advice to Congress or to help the President keep things running smoothly. Our first political task is to be the church, to keep criticizing our message, mission, and life together so that we become a people who are being formed and reformed by our dominant convictions.

The primary question is not whether what we advocate is effective, or acceptable, or practical. The question is whether or not what we advocate is true to the gospel. We best criticize the world by being the church, a people who belong to another King and his Kingdom.

When I was a boy, I read Charles Sheldon's little devotional classic *In His Steps*. It is a simple little book about a man who determined to answer all ethical questions in his life by first asking, "What would Jesus do?" Unfortunately, Sheldon generally implies that asking this question leads to a more prosperous, successful life. When I grew older, I read Thornton Wilder's funny novel *Heaven's My Destination*. Wilder, unlike Sheldon, seemed to have an appreciation for what happens to people who take the gospel seriously. Wilder's protagonist decides to live his life by the Sermon on the Mount. What follows is a series of uproarious episodes as this poor man is buffeted about by the circumstances he creates with his odd lifestyle. I particularly remember one scene in which he withdraws money from his bank account. An argument ensues with the teller, because he refuses to take interest on his account due to Jesus' strictures against usury. Other customers, overhearing the argument, assume that the bank is in trouble, and a run on the bank is precipitated.

In a way, Wilder had it right.

Christian social concern may appear foolish and ineffective to the world. Jesus himself appeared powerless and ineffective.

His power was the truth rather than worldly violence propping up falsehood. Our aim is not "effectiveness" but a prophetic demonstration that Jesus makes possible a new social order based, not upon what works or upon competing self-interest, but upon his lordship.

I thought of Sheldon's simplistic "What would Jesus do?" recently during a discussion in an adult church school class. The class had been arguing about capital punishment in our state. Some were in favor of capital punishment as a deterrent to crime. Some thought it was right as a principle of good justice. Others admitted that their belief in capital punishment was simply a matter of their own strong emotions.

"But what would Jesus do?" one asked. "Can you imagine Jesus encouraging his disciples to crucify someone else?" It was a simple, simplistic question, a question that showed little regard for the workings of the criminal justice system or the smooth functioning of society. But then, as someone else noted in the ensuing conversation, "Would Jesus be concerned about the criminal justice system or the smooth functioning of society?"

The question What would Jesus do? then led to a consideration of why Jesus would not do it. The group (and this was a group of uninformed laypersons, mind you) decided that Jesus could not support capital punishment, not because he was either naive or idealistic, but because Jesus tended to view the world different from Caesar. What might that insight imply for the followers of Jesus?

The gift of the gospel is, in great part, a gift of courage to see the world for what it is—a world ruled by powers and forces that derive their strength from our natural human fear of destruction and our natural need for self-preservation at any cost. Governments have gained such power over our lives because they offer us security in exchange for truth and freedom. Luther calls security the ultimate idol. We have demonstrated, over and over again, that we will exchange anything for a taste of security.

Membership in the colony of heaven gives us the possibility of freedom from these powers. We are given a vision of a reality that transcends the limits of this world, a vision that enables us to be honest about the impossibility of self-preservation and the insecurity of all our worldly securities. What else can the world do except build bigger bombs and pass tougher laws? Violence and coercion, legislative or military, are the only means the world has of transcending the human condition. This is why I expect that the current antinuclear movement will continue to be baffled both by the tenacity of the world's resistance to disarmament and by the cynical manipulation of the movement by politicians. In a world where there is no God save the one we create, no future save the one we construct, no hope save that which is based upon the possibilities for human progress, we are condemned to use whatever means are at our disposal for self-preservation. The bomb is the only ultimate transcendence we have—it will either keep everyone at bay in a delicate balance of mutual fear or else bring everyone down equally in nihilistic mass death and destruction. How naive of the church to ask the world to give up its gods, unless we first offer it something better to believe in. Having no God, the world will cling to its bomb.

None of this is a call for withdrawal from the world—such withdrawal is a sociological and theological impossibility. Rather, it is a plea to confront the world on our own terms. The pop slogan for the church in the 1960s was "the world sets the agenda." Central Church forgot who called the meeting. The gospel calls the meeting and sets the agenda. The world has done and will do anything in its power to avoid, subvert, or coopt this confrontation with the truth. So the church must never forget that the imperatives "come unto me" and "do this in remembrance of me" theologically precede "go ye into all the world."

In its very existence, the church serves the world, not by running errands for the world, but by providing a light to the world, that is, by providing an imaginative alternative for society. The chief political task of the church is not to provide suggestions for social policy but to be, in our existence, a social policy. As we said in the first chapter of this book, the gospel call is an invitation to be part of a peculiar people, a colony, an institution that is struggling to create those structures that the world can never achieve through governmental power and balanced self-interest. The world cannot achieve its hoped-for justice, freedom, and community. The church, by its very existence as a colony of heaven, is a paradigm for a society that the world considers impossible. The real validation of the Jesus story is when the world looks at us and says, as it said of our forebears in the faith, "See how they love one another."

Back in the 1960s, the church was often urged to get out into the "real world" where all the action was. But such a slogan raises the question of what reality is and who defines it. By the "real world," people often mean the status quo. Presumably, getting out in the real world would mean adjusting oneself to the reality of whatever happens to be the present condition of the regnant culture. For instance, one of my parishoners recently gave me a clipping of an article by a popular syndicated newspaper columnist. It was a column on abortion. The writer recounted how an infant died in a Chicago tenement from starvation and neglect. When police questioned the baby's mother, a fourteen-year-old drug addict, she told them that she never wanted to look after a baby in the first place.

The columnist went on to say that this baby's tragic death validated the need for more government-funded abortions, and exhorted all preachers who talk about the evils of abortion to get out of their ivory towers and into the *real world*.

But into what world would these preachers go if they were to leave their "ivory towers" (the columnist obviously didn't know any preachers)? a world where some people eat and others starve? a world where little babies die of neglect? What is real?

I asked myself that question during a recent coffee-hour conversation with a group of ministers. The talk had moved to the subject of abortion. One of the ministers said that he thought that abortion was immoral.

"Do you mean that you would ask a thirteen-year-old girl who got pregnant, God knows how, to raise a child by herself? Do you think that a thirteen year old is capable of being a mother?" one of his colleagues said. I thought of the story in the newspaper.

"Well, no," replied the antiabortionist. "I suppose there would be some extreme circumstances in which abortion would be justified."

"So what's wrong with a thirteen year old having a baby?" asked another minister. He was a black minister, pastor of a large black congregation in our town. "We have young girls who have this happen to them. I have a fourteen year old in my congregation who had a baby last month. We're going to baptize the child next Sunday," he added.

"Do you really think that she is capable of raising a little baby?" another minister asked.

"Of course not," he replied. "No fourteen year old is capable of raising a baby. For that matter, not many thirty year olds are qualified. A baby's too difficult for any one person to raise by herself."

"So what do you do with babies?" they asked.

"Well, we baptize them so that we all raise them together. In the case of that fourteen year old, we have given her baby to a retired couple who have enough time and enough wisdom to raise children. They can then raise the mama along with her baby. That's the way we do it."

I was reminded of the peculiar way in which the church views reality. In the world, what often passes for reality is dog-eat-dog, survival of the fittest, look out for number one, do your own thing, and the devil take the hindmost. But in the church, things will be viewed differently. Here, strangers become relatives; the weak are cherished; those who do not fit into the world's standards of value are baptized; and the poor are royalty.

Earlier I argued that the gospel claims make sense only when viewed as communal, corporate, ecclesial claims. Now we are reminded that Christian ethics appear nonsensical and incomprehensible to the world, because Christian ethics have an ecclesial base. They make little sense apart from the context of a believing, supportive, radical, obedient community of faith. Thou shalt not kill. Blessed are the poor. The last shall be first. Do not resist the evil one. Such ethics only make sense if there is a countercultural society that is strong enough to back up such radical behavior. The nonviolence advocated by Dr. Martin Luther King in the early civil rights movement only made sense as a countercultural phenomenon that arose out of the black church's attack upon the American system. Nonviolence was advocated by Dr. King, not as a useful tactic, a strategy for success, but as the peculiar way that the church radically confronts the world. Without such a church to support nonviolence, it is best to simply buy a gun and deal with the world on the world's terms.

So, as the rest of the world goes about disposing of the very young, the very old, the very weak, the very vulnerable, and the very poor and calling this "reality," the church adopts and embraces the little ones in the name of its Lord who loved little ones. The church remembers that it is not just to mirror the "real world" or to wring its hands. *The church is to prophetically create the real world.*

Thus we see why it is that for the church to be politically and socially concerned it must be congregationally concerned. The political question for us is, How can we form a community whose life is faithful to its central convictions? That is why this book about the church must be not only *de*scriptive but also *pre*scriptive. We must not only describe the church in loving detail, but we must describe it critically, as a people who are on the

Church as Microcosm of world

way to somewhere else—not merely a smug people who are content with where they are in their congregational life. Political questions like Where are our children? Do we honor the poor and helpless? What do we do with our old people? are appropriate social concerns for a church whose Lord bids it to ask such things.

It takes the church to keep reminding Christians of how odd is its peculiar vision of what the world should look like. For instance, political legalism is fine as far as it goes; it has been quite helpful in achieving many beneficial results in American society. But woe to the church that thinks this is going far enough. Governments, even the most benevolent of them, can never embody Christian social policy. As a case in point, the Constitution is based on the assumption that only by institutionalizing aggressive self-interest of the leaders, on the one hand, and the individual citizen, on the other, can internal conflict be avoided. In other words, the Constitution not only balances self-interest (you give me my rights, and I will give you yours) but encourages it (I must pursue my rights, or the whole thing is thrown out of balance).

This arrangement is fine when people have power they can put in the balance. But, as Stanley Hauerwas notes, it becomes particularly problematic when one is dealing with people who have no power.[6] If these people cannot secure enough power to enable them to voice their self-interest and enough power to vigorously pursue it, they are left out of the process. We only share power if it can be seen that it is in our self-interest to give up some of our power. Thus, conflict is inevitable, and some amount of coercion is essential lest the truly marginal members of a society disrupt the uneasy balance of competing rights the rest of us have established. It is also inevitable that the truly oppressed and utterly powerless of society are cast aside.

Hauerwas notes that our lives are destined to become more legalistic and bureaucratic, because we live in a social order that is individualistically organized. What we call society is little

more than an aggregate of self-interested individuals. Today,
American society is a kind of vast self-fulfilling prophecy: a society that is designed to work on the presumption that people
are self-interested tends to produce that kind of people.

"Nobody speaks up for us burned-out, washed-up, unem-
ployed, slobbering drunks," complained a parishoner of mine
as he wallowed in a drunken stupor from his alcoholism. "Us
drunks don't have any rights." Of course not. And why should
they? What "rights" has a drunk? What claim has this man on
our society? What can he contribute to the well-being of the rest
of us? Nothing. So he has nothing and should expect nothing.
American constitutional capitalistic democracy doesn't worry
much about the drunks.

This is why much of our so-called social concern is less than
Christian. By "social concern" we usually mean the politics of
power: Let us pass a few laws to give the less powerful a little
more power and don't bother about those who can't be given
any power at all.

The social legislation of the world can never serve the poorest
and the least powerful, the drunks of the world and their kin;
the best it can do is to give the less powerful a little more power
and call that justice. So the world cannot give dignity to the
very young, the very old, the very retarded, the very sick. For
the poorest of the poor and the sickest of the sick, there must be
hope that they are not dependent upon policy but upon the
promise that God's love is stronger than the forces of evil.
Nothing shall separate even the drunks from the love of God in
Christ.

Only the church can be the source of such radical hope, so we
must care for the world by forming the church around this truth
and no other. As Monika Helwig says, if it won't play in a cancer ward or a shoddy nursing home for the elderly then, whatever it is, it is not the gospel.

Hauerwas is right when he says that Christian charity is superior to political action and social legislation because, in its

traditional form, charity asks nothing of its recipient except that he or she be needy. Charity reaches out in compassion for no other reason and with no better goal in mind than that it is commanded to reach out by the Lord, a Lord who had compassion on the wretched of the earth and then commanded us to go and do likewise. Christians do not reach out to the poor because we deem them to be deserving, or in order to help them to help themselves, or in order to make future taxpayers out of them, or to keep them content and quiet. We reach out because we are commanded to do so.

Letting the Church Be the Church

In his book on the evangelization of the Roman Empire, the Southern Baptist historian Glenn Hinson concludes that Christianity defeated Rome simply because it outorganized the empire. The church gave the decaying Roman world a vibrant, tightly knit, exclusivistic organizational alternative to other secular communities. In its institutional life, the church presented the Roman world with a crucial otherness. It struck hard against the edge of something that was not grace, not kingdom, not justice, not redemption.[7] It was a church that well appreciated not only God's involvement in the world but also God's apartness from even the empire's best cultural achievements, God's "infinite qualitative distinction" (in Kierkegaard's phrase) from human society. The *Didache*, our oldest moral catechism, prepared candidates for baptism by instructing them: You will not kill. You will not have sex with other people's spouses. You will not abuse young children. You will not have sex outside of marriage. You will not abort fetuses. In this expansion of three of the Ten Commandments, the church put itself in a head-on collision with some of the Roman world's most widely accepted practices.

Not content to be relegated to the backseat status of a general religious influence on Western culture, the primitive church saw itself as something other than the world that surrounded it. On the eve of the fourth century, the church in Rome was feeding nearly twenty thousand of that city's poor, not as a social strategy, but as an outpouring of who the church is. It must have done so, not because it seemed to be effective by the world's standards or out of the church's general humanitarian concern, but because it wanted to witness to what its Lord was doing in and for the world. The church's social concern was seen as a means to sight, signal, and celebrate the coming of the Kingdom.

The church is the most neglected aspect of contemporary mainline liberal social concern. It is also the most neglected aspect of contemporary evangelism. People are urged by the contemporary Christian apologist to look into their hearts, or to be more successful, or to make an individual commitment. Rarely are they asked to be joined to the church as a necessary part of conversion. Perhaps evangelists are embarrassed by the present state of the church—and with some good reason. Or perhaps it is simply easier to preach a private faith, which is never challenged, to a political, communal formation that turns all other communities and political attachments upside down.

Thus, the actual existence of a committed, visible church is crucial for evangelistic and prophetic effort. We are rightly judged by the kind of people we produce. Once again, we are not talking about the church as it is, but the church as it is called to be, given our basic convictions. We are being prescriptive rather than descriptive. The church is always *in via* rather than *in patria*, its eyes set on a city not made by law and coercion, a city whose maker is God (Hebrews 11). The gospel call is a call to see and to be part of that polis.

This means that my task as an evangelical and prophetic pastor is to help the church think as clearly as it can about what we are to be. As Hans Küng says:

We are to preach *metanoia*. We must entice people from the world to God. We are not to shut ourselves off from the world in a spirit of as-

ceticism, but to live in the everyday world inspired by the radical obedience that is demanded by the love of God. The Church must be reformed again and again, converted again and again in each day, in
order that it may fulfill its task.[8]

As a pastor, I must ponder the communal nature of this conversion and its social, political consequences. Unfortunately,
our so-called social concern has sometimes led us to unconcern
about the state of the congregation. I remember a pastor who,
after two terms on the school board and an unsuccessful bid for
city council, was finally asked by his congregation to either take
care of business at home or seek other work. While he was busy
being socially concerned for the whole town, his own parish
membership dropped from seven hundred members to three
hundred. He explained the loss by saying that his more conservative members objected to his liberal political involvement.
But I never heard any of his members criticize his liberal social
opinions. I did hear them complain that he was insensitive to
people's needs within the congregation, that his sermons were
poorly prepared, that he never visited, and that he couldn't remember the names of his own parishoners. In a way, he was for
me the epitome of clerical arrogance: I had better forsake my
vocation and get out into the city to work for justice, because I
can't trust my parishoners to do it.

Our pastoral authority primarily relates to edification of
God's people, not running about doing nice things for the
whole town. Many of our national church boards and agencies
have found that "serving the world" (i.e., making pontifical
pronouncements from the safe confines of the church bureauc-
racy) can be easier than helping us pastors form a prophetic
church that challenges the world.

I couldn't say it better than Jim Wallis does in his book *Call to
Conversion:*

The greatest need in our time is not simply for *kerygma,* the preaching of the gospel; nor for *diakonia,* service on behalf of justice; nor for
charisma, the experience of the Spirit's gifts; nor even for *propheteia,*

the challenging of the king. The greatest need for our time is *koinonia*, the call simply to be the church, to love one another, and to offer our lives for the sake of the world. The creation of living, breathing, loving communities of faith at the local church level is the foundation of all the other answers. The community of faith incarnates a whole new order, offers a visible and concrete alternative, and issues a basic challenge to the world as it is. The church must be called to be the church, to rebuild the kind of community that gives substance to the claims of faith.[9]

Before we dismiss Wallis as hopelessly idealistic, let us be sure that we are not using "church" in too restricted a sense. Some may object that the church that is described and hoped for here does not exist, that the current church is as fragmented and immoral as any other culture-bound institution.

Once again, it is essential for talk about the church to be prescriptive as well as descriptive. The modest task of the pastoral theologian is to help the church think clearly about what it ought to be, what institutional arrangements are needed for the church's organizational life to reflect our basic theological convictions. The church may not be as dead as some people think. When we wring our hands over the state of the church, we usually have the Protestant church in North America in mind. But the church is wherever people form a community as a prophetic witness to the reality of God's Kingdom.

I personally believe that this witness is seen more vividly in churches other than those of North America—in Africa, for instance, where churches are self-confidently growing, suffering, and witnessing in spite of the surrounding social order. In our thinking about the church we must never accept as normative the limits of the church in our own time and place. God does not abandon the church but continues to provide a faithful witness to the Kingdom, even though that witness may be in a neighborhood other than our own. The church is an international body, a sign that God, not nations or economic systems, rules the world. In my opinion, Central Church and its adaptationist posture to the world will, and perhaps should, pass. I expect such acculturated expressions of the faith to go the way of other churches before them that sought to simply keep house within the status quo. Reading the New Testament, looking back to what the church has been even as we look forward to what it can be, I am impressed by the effort expended in helping the church to be the church. How seriously these first Christians took the task of making proper distinctions between the church and the world! They warned initiates that they had better be prepared for the shock of moral innovation if they planned to enter the church. These early pastors were determined that the church serve and convert the world without becoming a victim to its own astounding evangelical success. At a time when the church fought for its existence, it battled, not by reducing its witness to the lowest common denominator, but by making careful distinctions between itself and its world, so that it might be truly for the world by being radically against it.

Here is how a second-century Roman Christian described the church's peculiar relation to the surrounding world:

Christians cannot be distinguished from the rest of humanity by country or language or customs. They do not separate themselves into cities of their own; they use no special language; nor do they follow an eccentric pattern of life. Their doctrine, unlike that of many religious movements, is not based on human ideas or philosophy. Although they live in Greek and barbarian cities, depending on their place of birth, and follow the usual customs of those cities, they never cease to witness to the reality of another city in which they live. They share in everything as citizens, yet endure everything as aliens. Every foreign land is their fatherland, and yet for them every fatherland is a foreign land.

They marry, like everyone else, and they beget children, but they do not expose their unwanted infants to the elements. They share their board with each other but not their marriage beds.

They busy themselves on earth, but their citizenship is in heaven. They obey the laws of the land but in their own lives go far beyond the laws' requirements. They love all people, and by all people are

God?

persecuted. They are put to death, and yet they are brought to life. They are poor, and yet they make many rich; they are completely destitute, and yet they enjoy complete abundance. They are dishonored, and in their dishonor are glorified; they are reviled, and yet they bless. They are treated by the Jews as foreigners and are hunted down by the Greeks; and all the time those who hate them find it impossible to justify their hatred. To put it simply: *What the soul is in the body, that Christians are in the world.*[10]

Now, the church must focus again upon its peculiarities. Now, the church must see itself again, not as a baptizer of a culture, but as a political and ideological monkey wrench thrown into the culture. Our Lord's prayer for the church of another time could as well be for us today:

I do not pray that thou shouldst take them out of the world but that thou shouldst keep them from the evil one. They are not of the world, even as I am not of the world. . . . As thou didst send me into the world, so I have sent them into the world. (John 17:15–16, 18)

4. Acting Like Christians

IT ALL started harmlessly enough. A group of church women were looking for a service project within the community. Someone suggested that they might do something at the local jail.

Pine Mountain is a resort community with a wintertime population of four or five thousand that explodes to forty or fifty thousand in the summer. Over the years, Pine Mountain has become a favorite gathering place for thousands of high school and college students, who flock there on spring and summer vacations. There they drink, sunbathe, and carouse, and a good number of them run afoul of the law. A major part of Pine Mountain's revenues come from fines imposed upon youthful offenders, who pay dearly for public drunkenness, open display of alcohol, and an assortment of other misdemeanors.

The antiquated little jail at Pine Mountain was always filled with unfortunate youths awaiting bail or fines. Adding to the problem is Pine Mountain's popularity as a destination for youthful runaways. Runaways are picked up and indiscriminately incarcerated, because the jail is the only place in town for them to await a ticket back home.

So someone in the church suggested that it might be nice if a group of the church members made something for the people in the jail. Perhaps a toiletries kit would be good—a toothbrush and toothpaste, soap, shampoo, a piece of candy to make their stay a little brighter.

One of the women met with the jailer and asked him about it.

"It's not our job to make life soft for them," he said, "but I've got no objection to you ladies at the church doing a little something. Just keep it simple."

They set to work making the kits, one for men, another for women. Each week, a load of kits was taken to the jail by Florence Smith and Myrtle Thompson.

The first thing that impressed the women was the sheer number of prisoners—at least thirty a week. Florence discovered (in conversation with the city manager's wife) that the city collected over a hundred thousand dollars a year from its jail operations. She overheard jokes among the police about "filling my quota for the week" as they brought in prisoners for booking.

Myrtle told the women that she was shocked at how the female prisoners were treated. She heard the police making "suggestive comments" to some of the young women who were being held at the jail. Also, she was surprised that in the incarceration procedures no distinction was made between older and younger prisoners or first offenders and repeat offenders. She told the women that she was beginning to feel that "our city jail is a disgrace. It's doing more to encourage crime than to stop crime."

Meanwhile, the little kits were expanding. Someone ordered Scripture pamphlets from the American Bible Society to include with the toiletries. Grace Anderson's prayer group donated a quarter for each kit. The coin was placed in an envelope with a note that read,

> Use this to call someone who loves you, or call us.
> We're always ready to listen. We care and God cares.
> Christ Church: 277–3821

Myrtle said that the quarters and the notes were fine, but the prisoners were only allowed to make one call a day and that had to be made from 8:00 to 9:00 A.M. or from 4:00 to 5:00 P.M. If they couldn't reach their relatives at those hours, too bad.

"We can't spend all day watching them talk on the phone," was the jailer's response to Myrtle's inquiries about prisoners' telephone privileges.

"Why couldn't we volunteer to go down to the jail and super-vise the telephone for the prisoners?" said one of the women.

"Can you imagine a fifteen year old, first time in jail, who can't even call her mother to help her out?" another asked.

"We can organize ourselves," said Myrtle, "like we did for the fall bazaar. We can cover the jail telephone for the prison-ers. We could make calls for them, even. We could also help them get legal advice."

This is when the trouble started. When the women began spending more time at the jail, they saw things that few citizens of Pine Mountain had seen. They noticed the attitude of the po-lice toward their work. They saw signs of excessive force being used on prisoners. They heard rumors of money changing hands in order to get people lighter sentences.

"I knew we were asking for trouble when we let you women stick your noses into things," the jailer said when a delegation from the women's newly formed Task Force on Local Prisons met with him to ask questions. "You women ought to stay out of what is none of your business," he advised. "What goes on here is really no concern of yours. Why don't you stick to church work and leave the legal work to us."

"This *is* church business," shouted Myrtle Thompson as she pounded her fist on his desk. "And therefore this is a concern of ours. If we don't get good answers from you and if we don't get them fast, we are calling the State Law Enforcement Divi-sion to look into the situation here."

The jailer refused to cooperate. "You ought to stick to reli-gion, stick to saving souls, and let me handle the criminal ele-ment," he said.

"You're going to find out what a mistake you made when you began messing around with a group of Christians," Florence Smith muttered to the jailer as the meeting ended. "Some of our best friends spent time in jail."

To make a long story short, the police refused to cooperate. The women did indeed call the State Law Enforcement divi-

sion. They then drew up a formal complaint against the jailer
and his jail at their Spring General Meeting. An investigation
was launched. The city was charged with improprieties. All this
eventually led to the jailer's resignation. Things changed at the
jail.

This is a small example of what can happen when people begin messing around with the church. Christians, by simply being about their proper business and keeping their attention focused in the right direction, can be a light to a dark world.

What Is Morality?

Many people who think of the church picture it as a kind of
ethical improvement society founded by Jesus: "The purpose of
the church is to help us live better lives." In other words, the
church is a means to an end, an organization whose purpose is
to do some minor adjustment and fine-tuning on our lives. People frequently praise or condemn the church on the basis of the
behavior of its members. This is fair, but only insofar as they
understand the church's claims for itself as a moral community.

In earlier chapters we have challenged the utilitarian view
that the church is simply a helpful organizational means of
achieving some good human purpose. The church is an end in
itself, the visible result of God's gracious intercourse with the
world. The church exists, not to enable people to be better, but
because God wills it. Whenever the church is seen as essentially
a means of improving society, or producing better people, or
fostering a love of good music, or giving the youth something
wholesome to do on a Saturday night, the church is whittling
itself down to scale as one more human organization that is
content to be useful in doing things that other human organiza-
tions may do better.

The moral significance of the church is a more complex phenomenon; it is not simply a place to urge nice people to be nicer.
The moral significance of the church arises as a kind of gracious

by-product of a people who are first satisfied to be before they attempt to be good, a people who, in celebrating what God is doing in Jesus Christ, are surprised to find that God is doing something to them as well.

In this chapter we shall examine the church's role in Christian ethical life, how it can be said that the church contributed to the moral direction and motivation of the women of Christ Church who rattled the bars of Pine Mountain jail.

Capital punishment? Nuclear arms? Premarital sex? Divorce? How does a Christian decide what is right? Contemporary Christian ethics has often presented the moral life as a series of decisions. What ought I to do? is the question that characterizes the ethical dilemma. In deciding what we ought to do, we refer to certain principles, rules, and values, and then we decide on the basis of those principles. The purpose of ethics, in this view, is to keep us free enough, bold enough, and sincere enough to enable us to act on the basis of our convictions. Action that has no better principle to commend it than "I felt in my heart that this was the right thing to do," or "I did it because everybody else was doing it," or "It seemed the easiest way out," hardly qualifies for the designation of moral action. And so the ethical life is characterized as a life of thought, deliberation, development of conscience, and freedom of choice.

This view of moral activity has its appeal to the modern Western liberal mind. We like to picture ourselves as rational, deliberating, autonomous beings who are free to do anything we want. Under this point of view, decision is everything. Actions that are done merely "out of habit," or as "second nature," are not ethical, because they violate our notions of the sanctity of human reason and the necessity for us to act freely without the restraints of tradition, emotion, and other people's opinions.

If the best a person can offer in defense of his or her behavior is, "I did it because my mother taught me this was right," it is not morality at all. For us, the ethical person is an autonomous person (literally, self-law). We are laws unto ourselves. Tradition, habit, family, community, even principles and rules, cannot be trusted, because they tend to limit our individual prerogative and freedom of choice. And what is ethics but a matter of choice? If I am in circumstances in which I am literally not free to decide, I am not in an ethical situation. I must be free to make up my own mind and then to follow the dictates of my own conscience.

I must be free to develop and exercise my autonomy, my self-law, because I like to picture myself as among the first generation of people who have ever lived on the face of the earth. The past cannot be trusted, because our present moral dilemmas are so new and unusual that only present opinions count. The community is of little value, because it only stifles my freedom by forcing me to consider the unhappy possibility that other people see things differently than I.

Recently, in a national church magazine, there was an article criticizing a woman in Boston who aborted twin fetuses that were thought to have Down's syndrome. A reader responded: "How can you know the agony this woman went through before she decided what to do? None of us can say what is right in this situation unless we were there ourselves."

In other words, the respondent seemed to say, there can be no "right" or "wrong" in the abstract or even in the social sense of the words. Morality is a matter of individual choice in the moment without regard to any other social, political, or traditional considerations.

I suspect that reason itself is no longer a major factor in our moral activity, since reason, by its nature, has a public quality to it. We can at least have a public discussion about whether something makes good sense or not. This was the force behind Kant's categorical imperative—my individual actions in a certain situation ought to conform to what makes good sense in any number of similar situations when reasonably examined by other thinking people.

When someone argues that a person's individual "agony" made his or her actions just, we have exchanged the radical individualism of Kant's rationalism for the even more radically subjectivized individualism of personal emotions. In other words, ethics is no longer a debate over what is right or wrong but a matter of being sensitive.

The moral person is thus depicted as the autonomous, lone free agent who is cut loose from the former moral equipment of rules, reason, principles, tradition, and habit. Each dilemma must be approached with open-mindedness, intentional ignorance, and kind sensitivity, coupled with aggressive independence, before one asks, "What ought I to do?" Ethics becomes a psychological event. The moral self is viewed as an amazingly trustworthy, discontinuous decider and doer.

This view of morality has its appeal in both liberal and evangelical Protestant circles. Since its beginning, Protestantism has been the faith of individual conversion, personal conscience, antitradition and anti-institution. Protestant rationalism asks, "Does this seem reasonable to me?" And Protestant pietism asks, "How do I feel about it?" But it is all the same—my reason or my feelings as the test of everything.

All of this raises the question, What is morality? If morality is not simply a matter of following the rules, or of letting personal feelings or reason be one's guide, what is it?

The Making of Good People

What ought I to do? may not be the most pressing moral question. Who do I want to be? may be more to the point. Although decision and choice are important, so many of the "ethical" things we do or avoid doing arise, not by reference to a rule or out of agonized decisions, but simply out of habit. Our decisions arise from somewhere. The choices we make are interesting not only for their consequences but because of what our choices tell us about who we are and who we are becoming.

Moral life is not simply deciding this or that; it is a complex of factors that form us unto certain sorts of people who decide in certain ways because of who we are. Our actions flow from our identity. So we do well to inquire first, not into how we decide what to do, but how we become who we want to be.

Ethics Is a Social Phenomenon.   The woman in Boston, in deciding whether or not to abort the twin fetuses did not arrive on the scene of that dilemma as some lone, exclusively rational or exclusively intuitive free agent. She came with a history; she came out of an ethical community. All ethics is social ethics, the result of living in a social framework. We learn our ethics as we learn language, as incidental to growing up with certain people, not because someone sat us down and taught it to us.

The assertion that none of us can say what is right in this situation unless we were there ourselves, rather than discrediting the power of our moral socialization, proves that we have been socialized into the American system's values of freedom, individualism, self-reliance, and contempt for history.

Our moral lives are cumulative and social. Debate over "right," "wrong," "good," or "bad" is impossible except as a debate in the context of a society that values certain things more than others and that grows through experience. "Let your conscience be your guide," automatically forecloses ethical discussion and protects us from the scrutiny of the community. Religion, we assure ourselves, is "a private affair." How dare you question my motives?

The church is the social matrix where Christian ethics arise. We do not act like Christians by natural inclination because we are made, not born. We are formed into Christians in the crucible of the church lest there be any misunderstanding that this is a thoroughly social faith. Our minds are stretched through the tradition of the church; our moral possibilities are broadened; and our present actions are placed in a larger context than what merely seems right to us in the moment.

The women of Christ Church came to a head-on collision

with the jailer not simply becuase he was an evil person (which in a way he was) but because they had been socialized into a different set of values. They valued things differently than he did. Their community (the church) had taught them to act and react to certain things and not others. Their behavior was a social product.

Ethics Is a Matter of Habit.   Aristotle was first to note that it was too much to expect ordinary people to be good. About the most that one could hope for is that we might develop good habits. In our daily lives we do not agonize over most decisions. We do not steal, we do not kill, not because we have consciously decided on anything, but out of "second nature." These habits are no less ethical because they have become part of us; in fact, they are the very qualities that make us people of character and fidelity. "That's just what I would have expected her to do" is an everyday observation of habits that form character.

Now, to speak of morality as a matter of habit is to swim against the stream of contemporary thought. It implies that morality is not only the stunning, heroic choice but a more mundane, long-term, institutionalized, habitual, disciplined affair. We would rather think of ourselves as heroes than submit to the discipline and lifelong formation of a community. We would rather see our actions as discontinuous, *ad hoc*, and isolated than as cumulative acts that either weaken or strengthen our character. The disconnected Western modern man or woman— a mosaic of conflicting rules, a wardrobe of quick-change masks and postures, independent, pre-eminently adaptable, yet cut off, without a significant past or the slightest hint of the future—how could such a patchwork person answer, What ought I to do? The prior question is, Who, in God's name, am I?

For the Christian, ethics is not simply a matter of deciding what suits the situation, or even what seems right. Ethics is an expression of discipleship—disciplining our lives in congruence with our Master. The church does so many things ritually and habitually, because it senses that its vision is so odd, so

against the grain of the wider society, that only constant atten-
tiveness and lifelong cultivation of that vision will enable it to
endure in the lives of those who are Christ's disciples.

Morality Arises Out of Vision.   My actions are not simply a
matter of deciding between option A and option B on the basis
of past experience. Actions also arise out of my vision of the future. This vision gives life coherence and direction, even
though it may not specify the specific steps along the way.

Talk of right or wrong can only be meaningful in the context
of some vision of the sort of world I want to live in and the kind
of person I hope to be. So a person in Boston who agonizes over
whether or not to abort twin fetuses might ask not, "What
ought I to do?" but rather, "What sort of person do I want to be
at age sixty-four?" or the even more visionary and socially activist question, "What sort of society do we want in the year
two thousand?"

The images, stories, sacraments, and work of the chruch give
shape to the Christian vision, refurbish that vision in our people, and pass it on to our young. Without such vision, Christians might stop agonizing over what is right and true and settle
for well-intentioned kindness, or decency in general, rather
than Christian ethics in particular.

Life in the wider American society can never foster the countercultural vision that discipleship demands. The surrounding
culture has its own secular view of what ought to be, a vision
that is seductive to those who neglect the development of spe-
cifically Christian character and are careless about whose altar
they bow before.

In the church, we are urged to see things as they "really
are"—as the church defines reality. As we noted in the last
chapter, when people urge the church to look at the "real
world," the world that they are usually referring us to is the status quo. The church is the political lens through which Christians look at the world. There are moral consequences for a
people who define reality in terms of the last being first and the

first last, children being at the center of it all, and the poor, the hungry, and the sick being royalty.

This vision determines to a great extent what we see in reality. The Christian expects to see and say things differently from the non-Christian, for each will be employing different symbols of his or her world. The world uses metaphors like "non-productive," "quality of life," and "practical" in evaluating moral activity. These terms arise out of what a consumer-producer–oriented economy thinks important, and they limit its vision of what ought to be.

So the church is morally significant not simply as a place to learn the right rules but in a more dynamic sense as a place that urges us to look in the right direction. In the church's worship, our vision is sharpened, clarified, and given vitality. Thus the church is a place full of symbols and images, for this faith is so complex and rich that it cannot be apprehended save through the richest of metaphors.

We make Christians by telling them stories of bad little boys like Jacob who got saved anyway and about a Savior who came via a cow stable, and by showing them a cross and asking them to shoulder it, and reminding them, as did the women of Christ Church, that "some of our best friends spent time in jail."

It is difficult to specify how such visions inform morality, but we know they do. What happens to the couple deciding whether or not to end their marriage—or to the person dying of cancer, or to the teenager deciding what to do with her life—when these people come to church and a cross is lifted up as the central image of what this faith is all about, the chief symbol of our peculiar definition of salvation, and our odd way of measuring success?

In the church we gather to envision a "new heaven and a new earth" where the deaf hear, the blind see, and outcasts come to a feast. So, in a sense, the church contributes to the ethical life by focusing our ethical concerns upon something more adventurous than self-preservation and personal security.

Who We Are, What We Do

For Christians, the most interesting ethical questions are always theological questions. Our life is responsive. Our ethics are but the human response to God's reaching out to us in Christ. We begin any discussion of what we ought to do with the faith that God is with us. For us the truth is a person, personal. The gospel is not about love; it is about this man, Jesus Christ, who makes love possible. To be a believer in Jesus is not to affirm a set of noble ideals but to be in a relationship with this person.

We owe God faith, said Luther, not works. We owe our neighbor good works. Only by trusting God are we enabled to love the neighbor selflessly. You get good works from good people. You don't seek apples from a thorn bush, Luther noted. Christian ethics arise out of Christian faith. That is why Paul, in his letters to young churches, lists his ethical injunctions after his theological affirmations. First he talks about God, then with a transitional "therefore" or "because," he talks about the implications of God's behavior for our behavior. Paul believes that our actions flow from our being.

We do people great injustice when we mislead them into thinking that Christian ethical attitudes—Thou shalt not kill; Blessed are those who hunger; It is easier for a camel to go through the eye of a needle than for a rich man to enter the Kingdom of God—make sense, should be affirmed by all rational people, and would help America be a better place in which to live.

These attitudes do not "make sense" outside of the point of view of faith and the social support, habits, and vision of the community of faith in Jesus. Acting like a Christian is not so much a matter of thinking about an appropriate path of action and then courageously deciding to do it. Christian action is more like the matter of being in love with someone. When we are in love our energies are released, our attention focused, our goals redirected, and our whole picture of the world transformed.

Talk about thinking, deciding, and choosing fails to see that being in love is usually not something one decides to do. It is an attachment beyond the bounds of reason, command, and will. Iris Murdoch notes that we human beings are "attaching creatures."[1] We do not so much decide to be good or courageous as become attached to some object of love and attention that reinforces and releases our energies so that our good actions become, not an act of the will, but a response to the beloved.

We are obedient to whatever absorbs our attention. Therefore, the church is engaged in ethical activity whenever—in worship, prayer, education, music, storytelling, social action—it focuses our attention on the beloved (Christ). As Augustine said, "We imitate whom we adore."

Christian ethics is thus complementary to Christian worship. Both activities have to do with learning to pay attention. The church confesses that, until we are attentive to God, our selves remain mired in illusion, self-hate, self-defensiveness, and the anxiety that occurs when we assume that we are forced to create and sustain our own significance rather than its coming as a gift of God.

Sometimes the church gives us certain rules or helpful guides for behavior. Sometimes it gives us a forum for ethical debate and decision. It is right for the church to give its people help in discerning what it means to be a Christian. But the main thing the church gives us is God. That gift makes all the difference in who we are and what we do.

This is not to say that Christian ethics is mostly a matter of vague feeling or intuition. A believer related to Christ is related to more than a warm, nondescript, mystical being. The believer is related to a Jew from Nazareth whose life, teachings, and church form the specific content of this faith.

Sometimes we have claimed to know too much, easily identifying our programs of action with God's program. But the current pattern of moral life seems to claim to know too little rather than too much. Abortion? Nuclear arms? War? Marital fidelity? What can we know? God is so obtuse and obscure in revealing his will to us, we seem to say, we must take matters into our own hands.

Once again, as we said in the opening chapter of this book, the specifics of the gospel, its particularity, is its scandal. We have a stake in keeping our ethics vague, nondescript, and abstract, because that lets us define justice and goodness exclusively on our own terms. The church must keep us close to the facts of the faith, the specific customs of the gospel, the story itself. The women of Christ Church may not have known which specific steps to take in their journey into Christian ethical responsibility. Their tactics and methods could be questioned. They might have done other things at the jail. But their faith did point them in the right direction. It did necessitate their viewing some aspects of the situation as important and some as unimportant. It kept reminding them to take the side of the powerless in any dispute with the powerful. It assured that those whom the jailer regarded as the "criminal element" would be seen differently by the women who knew that Christ tended to view people differently than Pilate.

Morality is not something we switch on and off in specific situations when choice is demanded. Morality is a sustained product of discipline, a state of being that occurs between and prior to choices. Thus, the church must worry as much about the sort of people we are as about the choices we make. Christianity must not allow itself to become a moral system, with the religious reduced to little more than an emotional tinting, a vestigial accessory to an essentially humanistic ethical scheme. The religious, our relation to God, is the very ground of our ethics.

An example comes to mind from my own pastoral experience. After an Advent sermon on the story of the pregnancy of

Mary, I had the following conversation with a woman in my congregation:

Parishioner: I'm rethinking what I once thought after Sunday.

Pastor: What are you rethinking?

Parishioner: Well, you know how I've felt about this issue of abortion.

Pastor: No, I don't think I do.

Parishioner: I guess I pretty much followed the standard line.

Pastor: Which is?

Parishioner: Which is that it's OK—if the mother, if the parents, think it's the best thing to do.

Pastor: And you've changed? Why?

Parishioner: I don't know. It wasn't so much the sermon.

Pastor: Yes, I didn't even mention the topic in the sermon.

Parishioner: It was the Scripture, I think. When you read about Mary getting pregnant: her song, her joy, her vision about what God had in mind for her baby. I said to myself, "What do we think we're doing? This baby is what God wanted for the world. It wasn't our idea." It put me in touch with the birth of my children, the birth of children in the world—even poor children. Maybe I ought to say especially poor children.

The Christian acts in certain ways because of the Christian's constant encounter with a God who sees things differently than we do. Our ethics is our dangerous attempt to let God be God in the church, to keep taut the tension between creature and Creator, to, when making our choices, take God a little more seriously and ourselves a little less so.

Thus, the church is the central place of a Christian's moral formation, for only the church keeps this vision before us in this affective, habitual, social way. Christian love of God is not platonic love in the abstract; nor is it erotic love in the heat of passion. Moral formation is more like love in marriage—a life-long attention to the other in such a way that one is drawn out of oneself into the love of another.

In its stress upon instantaneous conversion and warm feelings, American evangelicalism shows inadequate appreciation for the depth of human sinfulness and places inadequate stress upon the long-term formation of the moral self. Discipleship takes discipline.

On the other hand, in its stress upon human decisions and actions and its confidence in the role of reason in behavior, American liberalism shows an inadequate appreciation for the persistence of human self-deceit and places inadequate stress upon the role of our communities in shaping who we are. We are not good enough to go it alone.

The church does not claim to have a monopoly on right action; nor does it presume to be immune from the same sinful human tendencies that infect all human behavior, even the best of it. The church's claim is that it sets us in the context where distinctively Christian existence and action occur. Knowing that so many influences upon our moral life have, on the surface, no moral impact, we must be attentive to the subtle forces at work upon us in church and in the world. The church, in its life and mission, keeps inviting us to venture forth from the cozy confines of life in post-Christendom America and meet the truth—not truth as a principle but truth Himself. Christ came preaching not love but discipleship. He was truth and love embodied, in the flesh. Discipleship is the tough business of learning to follow this Lord.

It is obvious that the church miserably fails to form people who consistently act like disciples. The church admits this and reminds us that we are sinners, no matter how long our tenure in the church. But it not only says we are sinners, it also offers us grace. In dealing with our failure to be Christians, the church sets us within the sole context of community, habit, and vision, judgment, story, and forgiveness whereby it is possible, even for us, to become Christians.

The women of Christ Church were not extraordinary ethical heroes or moral virtuosi. They were just ordinary people who had learned to pay attention to something extraordinary. They lacked sophisticated insight but possessed a profound spiritual vision. By their willingness to be fools for Christ, they confounded worldly wisdom and mocked the powerlessness of worldly power. They loved someone other than the world loves.

If we or the world could be saved through human kindness or clear thinking, Jesus either would have formed a sensitivity group and urged us to share our feelings or would have founded a school and asked us to have discussions. Knowing the ways of God, the way of the world, and the persistence of human sin, he took up the cross, called disciples, gathered the church, and bade us follow him down a different path to freedom.

5. The Bible: The Church's Book

AROUND THE family dinner table, we told stories. There was the story about the time that Uncle Charlie went to Chicago and ate at a fancy French restaurant. Then there was the one about how my grandmother and her sisters all came to be college graduates. There were stories about why our family always voted Democratic and why we were never to sell the land our grandfather had worked so hard to buy and farm. We told stories.

From these stories, I got a clue about what it meant to be growing up among these people, to bear this name, this history, this identity. The job of the old was to tell stories. The young were to listen, to emulate, to retell, until one day we would be able to live the story for ourselves.

The church is also a family living by stories. That's one reason why we gather on Sunday morning—to tell stories. All that effort expended in Sunday school, preaching, Bible reading, and much of our singing is an attempt to tell the story. We differ from Jews or Hindus or Moslems, in great part, because we tell different stories. A person can spend a lifetime attempting to figure out these stories. I've been at it for a few decades, and I don't fully understand them. I expect still to be surprised by them when I'm eighty.

Whatever a Christian is, a Christian is someone who tells certain stories about the world that strike us as a truthful account of the way things are. Whatever the Bible is, the Bible is our storybook. Its narratives teach us what to see, whom to value, how to live.

The Bible is our book; the result of Israel's and then the church's attempt to listen and then to speak to and about God. The church began in, not after, the New Testament. The Gospels and Epistles were the church's attempt to settle church squabbles and "discern the spirits," to pass the faith on to new converts and the young, to help the church be the church.

The converse is also true: The church is the response to the Bible. This is the narrative that, over the ages, has continued to form a peculiar people, a colony, a family. The church is the object of the Bible's most biting criticism and the Bible's most compassionate promises. Anybody may appreciate or admire the Bible. Only the church lives the Bible, uses it as Scripture, stands under it as truth itself.

Fundamentalists make claims for the Bible it doesn't make for itself; they begin with certain creeds or doctrines that they hold to be the abstracted essence of Christianity, then they claim biblical support for their presuppositions. They argue that the Bible is scientifically, or historically, true, that Jonah really was swallowed by a big fish and that Joshua really did make the sun sand still—thus making the Bible's truth dependent on the validation of science or history.

For their part, more liberal Christians admit that the Bible was historically conditioned. Using the techniques of biblical criticism, they attempt to unwrap the Bible's accumulated strata of traditions and recover the one original intended meaning of a text, event, or story. The Bible often has been picked apart until nothing could be said for sure about anything; the alleged one intended meaning for all time was rather small potatoes. The search for the original strata, though producing some helpful results, has proven difficult, if not impossible. Historical criticism sometimes has given us the impression that it could tell us everything a text didn't say.

Both conservatives and liberals often have read and interpreted the Bible in a way that is unfair to the Bible itself. Fundamentalists sometimes have seen the Bible as a repository of changeless, universal truths. Liberals, when they have used the Bible, have seen it as an uplifing, universally applicable guide to human behavior. Both groups have overlooked the Bible as the church's book.

The Bible is not a set of timeless creeds or universally applicable ethical principles. It is a conversation between God and God's community. It is a story that only makes sense within the context of a community that is dedicated to forming itself by what God says. The Bible is to be tested neither by science nor history but by the life of the church it produces.

The Flood

"When it rains, it pours," is how the saying goes. What's a person to do when he or she is knocked down by one blow after another? The psalmist speaks of these occasional times in life when we are buffeted about by the blows of cruel fortune: "Deep calls to deep in the roar of they cataracts, and all thy waves, all thy breakers, pass over me," (Ps. 42:7, NEB).

Jane was going through such a time in her life. Things had never been easy for her, but the past two years had really put her to the test. Her marriage to a moody, alcoholic husband had been increasingly unhappy. His drinking had become worse since the children had finished school and moved out. Jane's mother was her best friend and only solace in bad times. Six months previously her mother had died after a short illness. Jane felt alone, heartbroken.

Without her mother to comfort her, Jane found her husband's moodiness and drinking to be insufferable. In a fierce, ugly confrontation one evening after dinner, the floodgates opened and Jane's resentment, hurt, and rage poured forth upon him. She told him that he had made her life miserable, that she couldn't take it any longer, that he would have to change or she would leave him.

The next morning, without a word, he packed his belongings and left, taking their modest life savings with him and disappeared without a trace.

Two weeks later, I sat in Jane's living room as she recounted the events of the past months. She was broken by sorrow, tired, sleepless, anxious.

"They sometimes say, 'God never puts more on us than we can bear,' but I don't know now. I really feel that I've reached my limit, that I just don't have any strength left to fight or cope. I'm going down for the third time."

I told her that I doubted if God had put these burdens on her. But she didn't seem helped by my reassurances. I was fearful for her emotional state. With few friends to turn to, few marketable skills with which to obtain a job, she had good reason to be frightened about tomorrow.

"Curious," I said, "when I listen to you use the image of drowning to describe your situation, I think of an old story that we both heard as children."

"Which story?" she asked.

"Well, you say you are afraid that you're 'going down for the third time.' Are you drowning? Are the waves rising faster than you can tread water? I'm thinking of a flood, the story of Noah and the ark."

"Yes, everybody knows that one," Jane said. "Am I on the ark or outside in the mud?" she asked with a slight laugh.

"Where do you think you are?"

"In the water! Yes, that's where I am, going down for the third time," she replied.

"You remind me of when I was a child at the beach. I can still remember the rough surf buffeting me. Do you remember how each wave would knock you down, how as soon as you got back on your feet, the next one would come along and hit you?"

"Yes, so you eventually quit trying to stand up and fell back into the water and let the waves roll over you," Jane added thoughtfully.

"But you didn't drown, did you?" I asked.

"No, I floated. But I could always get back on the beach when I got tired. I'm not talking about fun at the beach, I'm talking about a flood!" she said in a sharp, angry way.

"Noah was in a flood. Can you recall that story?"

"Sure," she said, "God got mad at the world, fed up with people, so God sent rain, endless rain, which caused a flood and drowned everybody except Noah's family."

"Yes," I said.

"Great. That's all I needed," Jane responded sarcastically. "God is fed up with me, so God's trying to drown me."

"Do you really believe that?" I asked.

"Well, like you say, it's in the Bible, right there in Genesis."

"No, that's what *you* said was in the Bible. That's *your* version of the story of Noah and the flood," I said.

"Did I leave something out?" Jane asked.

"Well, yes. All you remembered was the part about the destruction, the water's blotting out life from the earth. But remember that God responds to the human corruption of the world not only by destruction but also by purging. Remember, Jane, water not only drowns, it also purifies, cleanses. God not only judges but also renews, enables the human race to start over, re-creates, begins again. There is the rainbow, the promise."

"I've never heard that story that way. All I could think about was the destruction," she said softly.

"That's understandable. There you are. So much that you hoped in, worked for, tried to put together is gone. It probably seems as if it's all destroyed, washed out."

Jane began to fight back the tears. I continued, "But I ask you again, where are you in the story? On the ark or in the mud?"

There was a long silence. Jane said through tears, "I don't know. I don't know anything."

"I know one thing, Jane," I said. "I believe that you clung to what you had, bad as it was, because it was safer for you to hold to that rather than test the waters. I don't like what's happened to you. It doesn't seem fair for someone who has as much to offer as you do to have this sort of luck. But maybe, just maybe, all this is being destroyed so that something much better can be born."

"I don't know," she said.

"Of course not. Not now. Neither did Noah when he stepped off the ark. He, like you, would have probably preferred to cling to the old world, bad as it was, rather than to risk the new. Nobody likes a flood."

"Well, I've gone down for the third time, but I'm not gone yet, am I?" she said wiping her eyes with a tissue.

"Good point! You are still floating, so to speak," I said.

"God, I wish I could know what I'm going to do tomorrow. Where will I get a job? How will I manage alone? Will I get married again?"

"I don't know the answers any more than you do, at this point. We'll have to wait. Like Noah. For 'forty days and forty nights' even. I don't see the rainbow yet."

"It's hard to wait. That's what has me scared. I just wonder how it will all turn out," she said.

"Right. It takes faith to wait. Of course, you've made it this far. You had good reason to go under, but you haven't. Now you're waiting for the clouds to clear."

"I couldn't have made it without God, without the church and their support, I'll tell you that," she said with determination.

"Ha! You are in the ark after all," I said.

Most of our Christian worship arises out of two sources, the Jewish synagogue and the family dinner table. What does a people do when it is exiled, homeless strangers in a strange land? It gathers and remembers, tells stories, celebrates its values.

What does a family do when it is caught in a hostile world? It gathers around the table for dinner. There, it shares food and love and tells stories.

Every Sunday, the church gathers before the pulpit and around the table for much the same reasons. The church consists of people who are determined to submit their lives and values to the force of the Bible. That day in my study, Jane was invited to submit her despair, her fear, her anger to the judgment of an ancient, childlike, profound story. I believe that Jane came to a new understanding of herself and her situation as a result of this encounter with the church's book. She recapitulated the movement, made so often throughout the church's life, of standing under the text, letting the story illuminate our stories, until we find both judgment and grace.

I responded to Jane's dilemma with metaphor, a story. I did so because I believe that the only honest work for today's preacher is poetry. I once thought that, as a pastor, my main duty was to be the surrogate activist for the congregation. I was to be out working, doing, changing parishoners and the world for the better. Today I believe that the hardest task for the pastor is *theoria* rather than *praxis*, vision rather than activity.

Christian faith is porous, free, visionary. I must be a poet to speak of this truth. The Bible is cast essentially in the narrative mode. Its domain is the world of image, metaphor, and drama rather than the flattened, modern, post-Enlightenment terrain of idea, program, strategy, and principle.

Liberal and conservative Christians expect their pastors to be teachers who give congregations moral instruction. The Bible becomes a rule book, a collection of sound doctrine or worthy examples. But this abuses the Bible. The Bible is basically, as we have said, a story.

Good stories don't give advice; they tease, surprise, shock, entice people. They show rather than tell. Good stories, as opposed to poor stories, help people *see*.

Poets keep people looking, wondering, envisioning. The significance of a good story can't be exhausted in one hearing. The story is sufficiently open-ended, ambiguous, porous, complex to be true to life. Homiletical and pastoral reductionism, in a misguided attempt to make it all easy, presents life as simpler than it really is. What could have encompassed the ambiguity and mystery of Jane's situation, what could have helped her to grieve without despair, to be honest without being cynical, other than a good story, with its subplots, levels of meaning, and double endings? Anyone who can't remember further back than the stories of his or her own birth is an orphan, bereft of memory, therefore without imagination, consequently without hope.

The preacher, the Bible teacher, the pastoral counselor, must know that we are battling for people's imagination. The purpose of the church, in great part, is to open the Bible in such a way that it forms an alternative structure of reality among the congregation. People are crushed, frightened, tied in knots, and timid because they have lost their vision, their imagination. They lack the requisite stories with which to make sense of their lives. So they cling tenaciously to whatever worldly consolation they can find.

The Bible bids us to look at an alternative story to the world's story, an alternative story to which we and our people will have ambivalent responses. In the world, Jane would be told to drop her faith questions, not to worry about the ultimate meaning of her life, and to pull herself up by her bootstraps as best she can. But the story suggested to Jane that God's grace continues, despite the flood, that God's good purposes for her life are born, rather than defeated, in tragedy. When the waves crash over us, our only hope is to fall upon the holiness of God. The vision comes by listening to the story even as we grieve over lost worlds. God has promised to uphold the created order, to stand with life against death.

Scholars tell us that the biblical story of the Flood did not inform the Hebrews about the deluge. The story of a great flood was common in the ancient world—it was perhaps a thousand years older than the biblical story of Noah—so a story of watery destruction was not news. What *was* news was the affirmation that God preserves the faithful, that human sin and natural chaos neither frustrate the purposes of God nor negate the promises of God. A distinctive feature of the Genesis account, as opposed to the Babylonian and Mesopotamian versions, is that the judge and the savior are one; the destroyer is also the creator. This ancient tale is thus retold in the faith community and placed in line with other stories of Adam and Eve, Cain and Abel, Abraham and Sarah, David, and all the recipients of the divine promise to make something out of this wayward people.

So we stand with Israel and look at the bow arched over the clouds, sign of divine providence. Because we have listened to the story, the church is able to be honest about the mud, the rising waters, the fury of the waves, the reality of destruction, for we have passed with father Noah, with Jane, with Israel and the church, through the waters, baptized into death and life, signed on our foreheads with the everlasting promises of a God who manages to be both holy and loving.

6. Preaching: Hearing Is Believing

IN 1347, a child was born in the large family of a Sienese dyer. They called her Catherine. Her family was poor but devout. Catherine was never taught to read; she never attended school. But as she grew, she viewed the frescoes on the walls of the cathedral in Siena. She saw there depicted scenes from the lives of the saints, men and women who courageously testified to their beliefs. Catherine felt that God was calling her to be a witness to the faith in her time. Beginning in her teens, she taught herself to read. By her early twenties, she was participating in the learned debates of theological scholars, astounding everyone with her gift for elocution. Her skillful oratory eventually helped restore the papacy to Rome and brought about many changes in the church.

In 1984, Jesse Jackson stood before a cheering Democratic National Convention and tried to explain how his life had led him to that point. As the son of a poor Greenville, South Carolina, unmarried woman and her next-door neighbor, it hadn't been easy for Jesse when he was young. But he remembered Preacher Sampson back in his church in Greenville, who told stories about the great heroes of the Bible, about people who had overcome adversity, prejudice, disability, and had triumphed. "He told us that we could be anything that we believed we could be," Jesse recalled. Sunday after Sunday the preacher told these stories, and Jesse listened—and believed.

This uneducated woman from Siena, this poor black man from South Carolina, heard something that led them to view themselves differently from the way the world looked at them. If God could use ordinary people like Samson, Sarah, Noah, Jacob, Joseph, Moses, Peter, Paul, then there's no telling whom God might use today.

It is upon such simple, holy hearing that God's saints are made, whether they be named Catherine or Jesse. That's the biblical definition of a saint: a saint is somebody who has heard the call of God in his or her life and said yes. The language of the church not only describes, it creates. The telling of the story keeps the story happening in our lives, keeps the Good News happening to us in our time and place. The church takes ordinary, everyday water, says Augustine, speaks the word, tells the story of how God has used this ordinary water at the Creation, in the dividing of the Red Sea, in the womb of a virgin, in the River Jordan, and we have a sacrament of how God saves us. The church takes ordinary table bread, says Augustine, and speaks the word, tells the story of how God fed the Israelites in the wilderness, how Jesus fed the multitudes, and broke bread with sinners, and we have a sacrament of how God cares for us. The preaching of the word creates the church, says Luther. Those of us who are in the church do so much talking and have heard these stories so often that it is easy for us to forget the power, the wonder, of the spoken word, the holiness of that moment when the preacher climbs the steps to the pulpit, pulls the chain on the little light, fumbles for a moment with sermon notes, clears the voice, and dares to speak.

Here is a faith born out of the dialogue between a people and a God who refuse to be silent. For the Jew, for the Christian, a chief wonder of the divine is that it refuses not to speak. Presumably, the Great God could have remained in silence for a billion years, doing whatever a diety does with eternity. But not, says Genesis, this God. Yahweh chose to speak. "And God said, let us create . . ." Sun and moon, fish and fowl, plants, all manner of creeping things, male and female came forth before the conversation ended. "And God said, 'It is good.' "

Out of the loneliness that only love can feel, God created someone to talk to—male and female, the whole buzzing, clicking, slithering, thunderous, roaring, gently rustling creation—partners in an eternal dialogue.

Time and again, according to the way the Bible tells it, when humanity has stormed off to pout like a spoiled child, or slammed the door in a huff like an angry lover, or hidden within the shadows out of shame, this loquacious God has come looking for us, come wanting to begin the conversation once again, come to talk it all out for the thousandth time, broken our silences in the name of steadfast love.

I once thought that the greatest temptation for us preachers was to talk too much. "Diarrhea of the mouth" was the disease that I heard we suffered from. I confess that often we talk when we ought to be listening. I admit that often we say more than we really know.

But lately I've come to think that silence is the greater temptation. In a relativistic world where truth is but a matter of who wins in the latest public opinion poll, where too many people pitifully cower in their corners because they lack the sense of vision or confidence that makes bold action possible, where all voices seem to blend into the boring, inconsequential, nondescript drone of the television announcer, perhaps we are again ready to marvel at the holiness of one human being saying to another what truth is.

When I was in seminary, I remember reading a score of books that foretold the doom of preaching in the church. Preaching was castigated as woefully one-way communication, authoritarian, archaic, and utterly unable to compete with the razzmatazz of "Sesame Street" and "Oral Roberts Presents."

Someone noted that most of these books were written by preachers, not laypeople! For the person in the pew, though preaching had its problems, particularly contemporary preaching that had lost confidence in its own value, it was still the very lifeblood of the church, the font from which belief springs.

To a modern American culture suffering from television over-load, starving to death on a diet of grinning hucksters and triv-ial sit-com images of humanity, perhaps the simple beauty and integrity of one person climbing a pulpit to testify before other people had to be rediscovered. People become fatigued by tele-vision's penchant for constantly exploding images before us but rarely stopping long enough to try to understand them. They want, more than ever, a coherent vision of the world, some way to see and understand, something that endures beyond the next station break.

In a recent survey of the American public, rather than the key to modern culture and the wave of the future, the people on television were judged to be manipulative, false, and motivated to do something sinister to the viewer. The average American, it would seem, looks at the talking head on T.V. and says, not, "Here is my key to the world," but, "I wonder what this person is trying to put over on me."

Thus, in an odd sort of way, T.V. may lead the way back into the old pulpit rather than the way out.

After the resurrection of Christ, after his ascension, in the confusing, heady days after these surprising events, a little group of believers gathered in Jerusalem to wait and to wonder what was going to happen next. They were there on the day of Pentecost. Suddenly, there was a sound from heaven; strange tongues were spoken, strange languages were heard and under-stood. All of these diverse nationalities came together as one. Out in the street, onlookers assumed that Jesus' disciples were doing the same sort of unseemly carousing and partying that had got them into trouble when Jesus was with them. "They are drunk again!" they said (Acts 2:13).

Peter, the one who had been unable to find his tongue when the maid in the courtyard questioned him the morning after the crucifixion, was now the one who spoke: "Men of Judea and all who dwell in Jerusalem, let this be known to you, and give ear to my words," Peter said (Acts 2:14).

Then, in a five- or six-minute sermon, Peter told everything he knew about the Good News. He told what had happened to him, what had happened to the people in the room that day, what had happened to the folk in the street, who, until Peter told them, didn't know that it had happened to them. He told them about Jesus of Nazareth, the one who had been crucified and killed but who now was loose because "it was not possible for him to be held" by evil and death (Acts 2:14–36).

Peter, who on so many occasions is the one who understood so little, on that day understood enough and said enough in that five or six minutes to change the lives of "about three thousand souls" (2:41) who heard the word and said yes.

In this simple dynamic of seeing, telling, hearing, and responding, we see the birth and rebirth of the church, the manner in which the church happens in the world over and over again. So when someone asked the great Indian missionary-evangelist D. T. Niles to define "evangelism," he responded, "It is one beggar telling another where to find bread."

The Trouble with Preaching

All those books that I read prophesying the demise of preaching were right. Preaching is old-fashioned, archaic, primitive. More than that, it's downright primordial. We have come a long way in human civilization, but we never get beyond the necessity of one person telling the truth to another. Christians preach out of the basic need human beings have to share with another human being something one has found that is good and true, and out of the basic mandate of Christ to go into all the world and tell what has happened.

Yet some years ago, Helmut Thielicke argued that the trouble with the modern church was its preaching. Many laypersons who sit through sermons on Sunday would agree with him. "I just can't figure out why there are so few good sermons," one person said to me. Preaching seems to be in trouble.

Laypersons sometimes express bafflement at why their pastors are not better preachers. On nearly every survey I have seen, when asked what task they most want their pastor to fulfill, the laity put preaching at the top of the list. But when they observe their pastor going about his or her duties, preaching seems to be near the bottom of pastoral priorities.

I remember my exasperation, when I got out of seminary and into my first church, at my parishoners' erroneous notion that I had spent all those years in seminary studying how to preach. For me, the study of preaching had taken a backseat to counseling, church history, theology, activism. Poor, uninformed laity, I thought. If they only knew what real ministry is.

Poor, uninformed pastor. Later I came to see that maybe the laity know what ministry really is. In too many churches, pastors are consumed with every possible activity except preaching. Laity complain about poorly prepared, sloppily delivered, halfhearted sermons. They keep coming and keep hoping. Every survey of the laity shows that they are still listening. What's wrong?

Perhaps now at last the truth can come to light. There are so many poor preachers and poor sermons for the simple reason that preaching is tough. Preachers, in the words of Leander Keck, "have displaced Sunday matters with sundry matters" because few pastoral activities are more difficult than preaching. Something there is in many preachers that would have them believe that preaching is outmoded, old-fashioned, unappreciated, and irrelevant. Better to believe that preaching is pointless than to admit I fail at the activity that is the very lifeblood of the church.

Preaching is difficult. A sermon is not a lecture, though many degenerate into that. A sermon is not Daddy or Mommy telling all the wayward children what to do, though we've all heard enough sermons that did exactly that. A sermon is not a matter of passing out new information, because, two thousand years later, what's new?

A sermon is an exercise of faith. We never get beyond that moment when Peter had to stand up and say what he thought had happened in the world. Preaching, perhaps more than any other pastoral activity, requires me to put up or shut up, to lay my faith on the line, to put my cards face up on the table, to call the world's bluff and show what I have or else pass to someone else who has something important to say.

And there is nothing easy about that. I would rather defer on questions of ultimate truth, pass to someone who is better equipped, better educated, more experienced than I. I want to wait until all the evidence is in, or another opinion poll is taken. But preaching will not let me slip quietly out the door. People are hungry for meaning in their lives They sit there, Sunday after Sunday, quitely stewing in their own despair, thinking, "If he has anything to say, for God's sake, let him say it."

I believe that we are all inherently theological creatures. All of use are asking questions about God, even when we don't know what we're asking. So we listen for a voice that speaks clearly. We yearn for a voice that speaks, not with the smug self-assurance of the demagogue, or the silky-smooth unctiousness of the huckster, but with the boldness of someone who has heard something decisive, so decisive that he cannot rest until he has told it to us. We listen for stories that are as complex as life, stories that ring true because they arise out of truth.

I confess that sometimes I wish they weren't listening. I can tell you, as a preacher, that I bear a terrible burden when people listen, really listen, from the depths of their souls.

Some time ago I was asked to speak at the baccalaureate service at a college in South Carolina. I hadn't thought much of the many baccalaureate sermons that I had heard, so I accepted the invitation with reluctance. What had I to say? I wondered. The last person these graduates want to hear today is a worn-out Methodist preacher, I thought.

But I accepted the challenge, really worked on my sermon. All that work seemed inadequate when the day of the baccalaureate arrived and I nervously entered the pulpit. I looked out on two hundred new graduates who seemed none too pleased that now a preacher was going to tell them what was what before they could get their degrees and get on with life.

I began to preach. I was mostly interested in my sermon, taking care not to lose my place and to deliver it with as much strength as I could muster. Then, well into the sermon, I looked out among my audience, and low and behold, they were *listening*, really listening. Anyone could have seen it in their eyes. You could have heard a pin drop in the auditorium as two hundred pairs of earnest, deadly earnest, young eyes were fixed on me, hanging on each word, penetrating me with their intensity.

What am I saying? I thought. Am I right? Will someone go home today and really live what I am only describing?

In one intense moment, I was heard—and that's more frightening than we preachers like to admit.

Any sensible, merely normal human being is understandably frightened by that kind of challenge. It is fearful thing to be heard.

Preaching is also difficult because of the nature of the gospel. In spite of what we smooth-talking preachers might lead you to believe, the truth, the truth that is Jesus of Nazareth, can hurt. I don't mean the fire-and-brimstone pyrotechnics of the conservatives or the carping, moralistic scolding of the liberals but simply the way the gospel penetrates our lives and challenges us to the very core.

In my last church we had a group of people who met each Thursday for Bible study. We studied lessons that I would then attempt to preach from the next Sunday. One morning I was leading them in a study of the Gospel for that Sunday, which was Jesus' temptation in the wilderness. I described the possible meanings of Jesus' temptations and then asked them, "How are we tempted today?"

A young salesman was the first to speak. "Temptation is when your boss calls you in, as mine did just yesterday, and says, 'Im going to give you a real opportunity. I'm going to give you a bigger sales territory. We believe that you are going places, young man.'

" 'But I don't want a bigger sales territory,' I told him. 'I'm already away from home four nights a week. It wouldn't be fair to my wife and daughter.'

'Look, we're asking you to do this for your wife and daughter. Don't you want to be a good father? It takes money to support a family these days. Sure, your little girl doesn't take much money now, but think of the future. Think of *her* future. I'm only asking you to do this for *them*,' he said. Now that's temptation."

It hit me. It's tough out there. And we preachers ought not to make it sound simpler than it really is. Jesus knew, with the world the way it is and the gospel the way it is, many turn back who first put their hand to the plow, some turn away sorrowful, and conflict between one good and another is inevitable.

As a young preacher I thought that there weren't more prophets in pulpits because preachers were cowards. The way I figured it, preachers were afraid to speak out for fear that they would lose their jobs. Later, I came to see that this was not so. What keeps preachers from speaking the truth, the reason we often take the safe way out and make it all sound sweeter and easier than it is on Sunday morning, is that we have come to love these people we serve. It is tough to say unpleasant things to people we have grown to love.

So congregations must be warned against the homiletical tendency to divorce Sunday morning from Monday morning, our terrible need to tie it all up with a neat bow and make it all appear easier, less challenging, less demanding, less open-ended than the gospel really is.

Congregations must also be warned that they may not want good preaching as much as they say. Presumably, Jesus was quite a preacher. But he appears to have preached *away* more people than he won. He did fine in his inaugural sermon at his hometown synagogue in Nazareth, until he turned the tradition on itself and started claiming that these ancient words were being fulfilled this very day (Luke 4). Jesus was led to the cross, in great part, because of something he said that was not palatable to the congregation.

Presumably, "good" Christian preaching might elicit the same response today. We are, the Bible says, sinful creatures who filter out what we hear, subconsciously hearing some things and ignoring others. Let the pracher's words touch us where we live, hit us at the core of our souls, and the defenses and hostility begin to rise.

Jesus stood up in the pulpit in Nazareth and simply quoted Scripture and told them a couple of stories that they already knew—and set all of it right where they lived. Their response was, "Wait a minute! Isn't this the carpenter's boy? Who does he think he is?"

A friend of mine carried out a research project for a doctoral degree in which he tried to measure the effect of preaching on a congregation's racial attitudes. He devised and administered a questionnaire that measured people's racial beliefs. Then he preached a series of sermons in which he used the Bible, Christian history and theology, and all of the homiletical skills at his disposal to convert the congregation from its racism. At the end of a four-sermon series he administered the questionnaire again. Result: The congregation was notably more racist *after* the sermons than before!

Of course, you know why. His preaching, rather than converting them, had only uncovered their deepest prejudices. He had driven them even deeper into their thoroughly entrenched attitudes. Would you call his preaching a failure? If by failure we mean the preacher's inability to move his congregation from point *A* to point *B* in improving their racial attitudes, we would have to say that he failed. But if the purpose of the sermons was to simply confront people with the truth, then perhaps the sermons succeeded. The truth not only sets us free, as Jesus said, it also hurts. The truth, Jesus notes, can turn father against son, mother against daughter, brother against brother.

I preached as a pastor of a small Southern church, and people sometimes said, "If you were older you would understand . . ." or "If you were not a preacher and lived out in the real world, you would know . . ." I preached in a university chapel, and they said, "If you were not an intellectual at a university and lived in the real world you would see . . ." We today are also liable to ask the question, "Is this not Joseph's son?"

The same human defenses and warped perceptions that were at work in the good synagogue-going folk of Nazareth are at work in us good church-going folk today. Some preaching is boring, inconsequential, ill-conceived, and trivial. But some preaching is so good that it hurts.

I will spend all week visiting the local hospital, run for the local school board, coach the girls' basketball team, fill out denominational reports, call meetings about the state of the church's roof, play golf, or do anything else to keep from having to stay in my study and do business with the gospel and life. Any preacher doesn't need to look far to find reasons not to preach—and none of the reasons have anything to do with preaching being unimportant or outmoded. They have to do with the nature of being human and the nature of the gospel itself.

Perhaps the amazing thing about preaching, when you think of all the things that preaching has against it, is not that there are so few good sermons but that, in a relativistic, timid, myopic world, there are any good sermons at all.

Hearers and Doers of the Word

And yet, in spite of all the good reasons why there are not more good sermons and in spite of the many more good reasons why there are so few good hearers, sometimes a word is heard. Someone is challenged all the way to the tip of the soul;

the world is torn apart and reconstructed in such a way that that person can only turn around and be converted or else live embarrassingly out of step with the way he or she clearly sees the world to be. On those all-too-rare and utterly holy occasions, let the church point and say, "Here, this is what we mean by evangelism, by preaching the Good News. Here it is, over here in this person's life. This is what first gave us birth and keeps us going even today."

Some years ago, at a church I was serving then, there was a young woman whom I will call Anne. After college Anne had enrolled in pharmacy school. From time to time she came home to visit and worshiped with her mother and father.

One Sunday evening after one of her visits, I received a telephone call from Anne's father.

"Do you know what's happened?" he asked. "Anne just called us to say that she has decided to drop out of pharmacy school."

"Really?" I exclaimed, "what on earth is leading her to do a thing like that?"

"Well, we're not sure, preacher," he said. "You know how much Anne likes you. We thought that maybe you could call her up and talk some sense into her."

I told him that I would be glad to do what I could. I called Anne. I reminded her of all her hard work, her achievements. I urged her to think carefully before throwing all this away. "How in the world did you come to this decision?" I asked.

"Well," she said, "it was your sermon yesterday that started me thinking. You said that God has something important for each of us to do, in our own way. I thought to myself, 'I'm not here because I want to serve God. 'I'm here to get a job, to make money, to look out for myself. I'm going to get out of here and get in the same meaningless rat race as everybody else.' Then I remembered that good summer I spent working with the church literacy program among the migrant workers' kids. I

really think I was serving God then. I decided, after your sermon, to go back there and give my life to helping those kids
have a chance at life."

There was a long silence on my end of the telephone.

"Now look, Anne," I said at last, "I was just preaching."

7. Common Prayer

FEW AREAS of church life seem as strange, to the outside observer, as our worship. It's all so archaic, so odd. Christians gather and bathe, sing, eat, and drink. One can see them on Sundays, listening to long sermons, sitting in rows of pews, dancing, shouting, shedding tears. "What's the point of it all?" asks the outside observer.

What's the point of it all? means, to the modern man or woman, What good does it do? There, right there on a Sunday morning, we stand at the very center of the church. All else radiates from that point, like rays of the sun. There is the source of all that the church is and does. This has it been for the church from the first. In the second century, an early Christian writer describes church on Sunday:

On the day which is called Sunday, all who live in the cities or in the countryside gather together in one place. And the memoirs of the apostles or the writings of the prophets are read as long as there is time. Then, when the reader has finished, the president, in a discourse, admonishes and invites the people to practice these examples of virtue. Then we all stand up together and offer prayers . . . when we have finished the prayer, bread is presented, and wine with water; the president likewise offers up prayers and thanksgivings according to his ability, and the people assent by saying, Amen. The elements which have been "eucharized" are distributed and received by each one; and they are sent to the absent by the deacons. Those who are prosperous, if they wish, contribute what each one deems appropriate; and the collection is deposited with the president; and he takes care of the orphans and widows, and those who are needy because of sickness or other cause, and the captives, and the strangers who sojourn amongst us—in brief, he is the curate of all who are in need.[1]

But what's the good of it all, the modern woman or man wonders. The preacher steps from the pulpit, the ancient book is closed, the benediction is given, the Threefold Amen is sung, and the congregation scatters. What good did that do? The world still suffers. There are still poor to be fed, wars to be ended, and the general pain of being human to be endured. Was this hour of worship only a fantasy trip, an escape, a time to do what the church is often accused of doing—sailing out into the never-never land of its dreams rather than confronting the facts of life?

Many responses might be made to these questions. Some might respond that worship does motivate us to go out into the world to set things right. They point to worship as a time of withdrawal so that we might return refreshed and strengthened to do good.

It's true that sometimes worship does motivate and strengthen us. But this doesn't really get to the heart of the matter. After all, a good lecture might do the same. A political speech during a party convention might be a good deal more motivational than a few verses of hymn number 93.

At the heart of the matter, when one really looks at worship, one notes that, for all the good and useful things that might flow from it, it has a kind of uselessness about it. If we are in church on Sunday for a lecture, or a performance, or a concert, or a pep rally, we'd best go elsewhere, because none of these functions are at the heart of what we do on Sunday. In fact, Sunday is—when you get right down to it—nonfunctional. Worship, Christian or any other, has a scandalously gratuitous quality to it. People seem to do it for the sheer fun of it.

At its best, Sunday morning is not "working out" in the manner of the grim jogger who trudges past my home in the morning, sweating and groaning in order to live longer. Sunday is the person running to meet her lover, the child dancing wildly around the room when he hears there is a circus in town. That's the sort of "work" we do on Sunday. For Christians worship is an intrinsically valuable experience, gratuitous. It is its own reward.

This explains why you may have noted that people in worship are prone to excess. They may shout, clap hands, fall over in a faint, weep, or become angry and storm out before the sermon ends. Invariably, when people are building their houses of worship, they build them bigger and better than they need to be.

Returning to our proverbial "outside observer," he or she may remark, "Yes, and what does this extravagance show? It only shows that people are engaging in primitive propitiation or atonement or some other psychological activity in their worship. They do all these things in order to get something else. Besides, you Christians ought to be ashamed to be living in such fine churches. Whatever happened to your Lord's concern for the less fortunate?"

Here our "outside observer" has raised some serious objections. The first is not so troublesome, because we can easily show that, if all these Christians are doing with these fancy buildings and vestments and gatherings is propitiating the deity for their neurotic guilt, they are overdoing it a bit. Their worship has ceased to be cost effective by nature of its sheer extravagance. They could get cheaper, more effective relief in an hour of psychotherapy. We must still confront the utter extravagance—material, emotional, and spiritual extravagance.

Of course, that's the way love is—extravagant. If our "outside observer" were to stand in a lovely city park on a Saturday afternoon in spring, that's what he or she would see—extravagance. People who are in love tend toward extravagant behavior. They will sing, write poetry, acquire new wardrobes and hairstyles, cry, shout, dance. That's the way love is. In any of its forms, love is excessive. The starry-eyed teenager, the dozen red roses (now what good do they do anybody?), kissing—they are all part of loving excess.

The question, What good does that do anybody? will appear laughable to lovers. It's the wrong question to ask of the singing, kissing, dancing, laughing. It shows that the questioner is already on the wrong track, that he or she could not possibly understand what it means to be in love.

So here we are at the very heart of it all. Here is the scandal of Sunday morning behavior: We love because we have been loved (1 John 4:19). Our alleged excessiveness in worship is the excess produced by love. The church's worship on Sunday is a way of being in love. If you have never been loved by anybody, you will have difficulty understanding what the church is up to here (though perhaps it will not be impossible). But if you have been loved, you already know something of how lovers need to return love. You are already on the way to understanding irrational, nonutilitarian, gratuitous, delightfully useless behavior like Christian worship.

The faculty was discussing a proposal to renovate the seminary chapel. An architectural designer had been asked to turn this bare room of fading carpet and broken furniture into a more fitting place of worship. Nothing resulted from the discussion, though. Meaningful debate ended when one faculty member asked, "With the poverty and hunger that exists in the world, how can we, as Christians, justify spending fifty thousand dollars to pretty up the chapel?"

I noted that this person failed to offer a similar ethical objection when faculty salaries were raised each year; nor had I heard him question the morality of the luxurious (compared to the dusty chapel) faculty meeting room. It seemed poor taste for a person in an endowed, tenured chair to be straining at this aesthetic gnat.

I moved that we give to the poor the salaries of all senior faculty members, along with those of the dean and associate dean. Motion defeated. Of course, you and I know that such talk is not serious. It is only posturing that masquerades as a deep concern for the poor. The notion that the church's infrequent struggle for artistic excellence is the enemy of our sporadic quest for social justice is but one of the ways we avoid the demands of the Kingdom.

The very foundation of any persistent Christian commitment to human liberation is our keeping taut the tension between the world as it is and the world as God intends it to be. Failing at that, about all we can do is to point to the world as it is and feel guilty. We then urge John-the-Baptist-style fasting in lieu of genuine engagement with the world and characterize anyone who would dare throw a banquet or a wedding feast as a sinfully insensitive prodigal who doesn't give a rip for the poor. The charge against Jesus was not "this man is a social revolutionary" but "behold, a glutton and a drunkard" (Matt. 11:19).

The outside observer asks Jesus, "With the world in the shape it's in, why do your disciples build churches, carillons, stained glass windows; pay for sculptors, musicians, painters; wear woven robes, drink from a hand-turned chalice, and place real flowers on their altars when plastic ones would do as well for less money?

It was the Devil, rather than a prophet, who tried to convince Jesus that we live by bread alone; anything else, according to Satan, is sinful excess (Matt. 4:1–4). The Devil said this to one much poorer than I, living in a world more tragic than mine. Jesus' rebuke suggests that, for the Nazarene, bread is not the sole justice issue.

You and I live in a pragmantic, no-nonsense, capitalist society that has always believed that you can't have both beauty and productivity, creativity and utility. In such an environment, social problems are bound to be oversimplified as straightforward, materialistic matters; human need is reduced to bread alone; human beings are caricatured as stomachs, without ears or eyes, that consume, consume. Rather than dream or sing about what ought to be, we are urged by our society to adapt to the status quo and keep producing and consuming.

It's no wonder that art and cultural development are low budget priorities if judged in purely capitalistic terms; nor is it surprising that censorship of art is one of the first acts of totalitarian regimes. Marxist or capitalist keepers of the status quo, oppressors of the human spirit, see art as mere state propaganda at best, needless decorative excess at worst. They dare not permit such flights of the human vision. Keep people focused on the status quo as the only possible reality and bread alone as the only valid human concern.

So back to the question. "With the poverty and hunger of the world, how can we, as Christians, justify spending fifty thousand dollars to pretty up our chapel?"

A possible reply: Rather than a wallowing place for the guilty, the church is called to a much bolder, morally more risky task—to sign, signal, and witness the advent of a Kingdom, a countercultural place where the prisoners, the poor, and the wretched of the earth are royalty. Our sacraments and ordinances, our bathing, eating, drinking, and singing are not simply a sign of the coming Kingdom but also a manifestation of its presence. Here that Kingdom becomes tangible and visible. The phony dichotomy between the gospel vision of a just world and the gospel imperative to do justice in this world must be challenged. It serves only to weaken our energy for doing justice by either reducing the breadth of our vision or reducing our concept of human need.

After we have wrung our hands over the comparative pennies we spend on festal and artistic "excess" in our churches, we still must explain the extravagance of churches in developing countries. Why do people who are, by our standards, so poor build such fine churches? One liberation theologian I know sees this phenomenon as evidence of the ignorance of the poor and the need for "consciousness raising." This seems to me an arrogant idea.

In one sense, the poorer a person is, the more bleak his or her situation, the more he or she needs the liberation that only the parade, *la festa*, or a fine, well-sung liturgy can give. In my world, we Christians are comfortable with our dry, buttoned-down, Puritan rites; we are quite pleased with the world as it is and see no need to look beyond it.

The finest buildings in most towns are not churches, but the new federal building, the courthouse, and the general hospital—but then, most towns worship saviors other than the one who was criticized for his partying. Why do the poor throw parties, festivals, and "extravagant" liturgies except that those who live in the pain of real poverty have found the social and spiritual healing that comes from such "excess"?

I once questioned a friend, a black Baptist preacher, about how his church could justify the expenditure of nearly half a million dollars on church renovation in the midst of one of the poorest neighborhoods in town.

"You white folks just can't stand to see somebody like us let loose, can you?" he said. "That church is going to be our protest that it wasn't God who condemned us to living with this ugliness. That new church will be a sign, a revolution toward reality."

As we have asked in an earlier chapter, What is real? What constitutes reality in the Kingdom vision? It isn't the gospel that has made us contemptuous of style, beauty, the work of human creativity, song, dance, and festivity. It is our flattened, drab world that robs us of our vision and calls the resulting gray, pre-fab landscape real.

This first hit me when I was traveling in Italy and encountered some of the Byzantine era churches there. Their exteriors are usually drab, not too different from the surrounding warehouses and apartment buildings. But when one enters the church, as the eyes grow accustomed to the dim interior, a riot of color emerges; glistening walls and ceilings encrusted with mosaics dazzle and confound. I realized then that there was a time when the church bid people to withdraw from the illusory world where Caesar rules and the poor are oppressed and the sick and hungry are nobodies and enter the *real* world, where the first are last and the last, first, and the poor are royalty.

This is the "function" of the delightfully nonfunctional world of Sunday worship—*to withdraw to the real world where we are given eyes to see and ears to hear the advent of a Kingdom that the world has taught us to regard as only fantasy.*

What is real? That's what Christians want to know on Sunday morning. The church's mission is not only to care for the poor but also to turn with them toward a God whose love frees us from all that enslaves us. The vision that the church represents to the world is no small matter. It is a vision beyond the passage of a few more just laws, beyond obtaining a little larger piece of the materialistic pie; it is a sight that is a little more important than the government's latest economic program.

Only constant reiteration and renewal can sustain this vision. Sunday worship—the vestments, anthems, banners, processions, gospel choirs, mariachi bands, colored windows, and soaring buildings—is the primary way we sustain this vision of a new heaven and a new earth against the principalities and powers that would dull our sight. Any church that dares to care, *really* care, for the oppressed and to fight the ugliness of oppression will find that this Sunday morning "excess" of a once-timid church has now become its prophetic necessity, a "revolution toward reality" rather than aesthetic flights of fancy.

The world too easily captures us. We become blinded to the real situation of society now that God has come. Paralyzed by its givens, I become a prisoner of the status quo rather than an adventurer who is always pushing against the boundaries of the known world, daring to launch into unknown space.

To return to our analogy of worship and being in love: Romantic love involves momentary, sporadic encounters. But if this love is to last and deepen through time, it must eventually become habitual, ritualized. There must be a series of loving gestures and words that become a regular part of the lovers' lives. Show me a couple who decides to kiss one another only

when they deeply feel the need in their souls, and I will show
you a sick relationship. Most good marriages know that we
must do certain things together out of habit—like kissing, saying "I love you," spending time together, taking turns washing
the dishes. The habitual quality of these actions makes them no
less important than if they were spontaneous.

Thus we see why Christian worship not only tends toward
excess but tends also toward ritual. We keep doing these things
over and over again on Sunday morning because we know that
if we didn't we might lose our love. In fact, those times when
we don't feel like it, when we really feel no deep attachment or
desire to worship the Beloved, are the times we ought to be sure
and worship. So often on Sunday morning we come proclaim-
ing, "Lord, I do believe. Help the little faith I have" (Mark 9:24,
Jerusalem Bible). We come feeling our relationship with God is
weak and shallow; then, in the ritual, the singing, the words of
Scripture, the familiar friends and setting, we go forth strengthened, having grown in our love.

I have met those who feel that the ritual nature of worship is
a hindrance to the spiritual life. They protest that we should not
worship "unless we really feel it in our hearts." But this is a
very naive view of human nature and of what it's like to be in
love. A husband and wife do all sorts of things with and for one
another whether they really feel like it or not. They know that
it's important to keep at love, to keep working at the relationship even in those times (*especially* in those times) when we
don't feel like it.

The Establishment of any age or any political persuasion is
suspicious of such festivity. Jesus was put to death by those
who feared a riot among the people. The first Christians were
dismissed as being drunk. John Wesley was excluded from English pulpits by those who warned of his "dangerous enthusiasm." In any form, enthusiasm, (literally, "filled with the Spirit") is a threat to the Establishment. Marxist or capitalist
defenders of the status quo tremble when people let loose.

Laughter or tears, much less processions and parades, are feared by governments whose only interest is control.

About the best that the powers that be can manage in the way of festivity are a few bread-and-circuses pageants that are designed to keep the masses quiet, their bellies full, and their wills submissive. *La festa* will be little more than a time to get drunk, forget the pain, and escape from the world into a stupor of self-indulgence. Christian celebration is a protest against such ersatz festivity. Our worship arises out of our knowing something that the world does not, namely that Jesus Christ is loose in the world, bringing all things unto himself. Our festal excess is our faithful response to the way things really are now that this stunning word of God is known: I'll be there for you.

How tragic that in many of our churches our worship has become only an extension of the same cold, lifeless going-through-the motions of the dominant social class. We have transformed our churches from beachheads into fortresses. We forsake the rituals of festivity and sacrament for the obsessive-compulsive round of bureaucratic business, the long lists of programs, basketball games, choir practices, and finance committee meetings. Keep the people busy going to meetings and setting and evaluating goals rather than looking for the Kingdom. Rather than being a sign pointing toward the Kingdom, we can beome a roadblock constructed by a professional caste of clergy who are themselves drained by the inconsequential demands of a church that has forgotten how to throw a good party. Alas, our worship is distinguished more for its dogged persistence than its beauty and flair. We sit in our bolted-down pews, staring into the void like people next to one another on a bus. Sunday worship becomes a testimonial to our intention, not to cut loose from the world, but to protect the world from the action of the Spirit. How miserly, how niggardly, do we celebrate the sacraments—a wafer and a minute, individual glass of wine for a meal, a few drops of water for a bath. We preachers expend more effort keeping everything tied down and everyone under control in worship than we do helping people to become visionaries and celebrators.

So back to our outside observer. Just as outside observers are often incapable of judging the strange antics of lovers, so are they incapable of fully understanding what we are up to on Sunday morning. Whenever the church cuts loose and becomes emotionally extravagant, this excessiveness is our way of being in love and, by our love, being a sign, a signal, a witness to the advent of a new heaven and a new earth. To anyone who will listen we shout that "Christ loved the church" (Eph. 5:25). His love becomes the source, the reason, for our worship. His love explains the worship of the church.

Matthew tells the story of a woman who took a bottle of expensive perfume and poured the whole thing over Jesus. The disciples were quick to criticize Mary for her mixed-up priorities.

"What a waste," they cried. "She could have taken this perfume, sold it for a large sum, and done something useful with it—like giving money to the poor."

Jesus, preparing to go to Calvary and do something really excessive for the poor, told the disciples that it was they who had misplaced their priorities. Wherever the gospel story is told, Jesus predicted, the ever-present poor shall praise such "excess."

8. Priests Everywhere

IF I had my way, I probably wouldn't be here. That is, I wouldn't be here as a pastor. I would have been quite content to sit more or less quietly in the third pew from the front rather than be here in a pulpit, with open Bible before me, attempting to preach the gospel and lead this flock toward the Kingdom.

I came to Northside Church the same way that I have come to every church where I have served—I was put here. A few years ago the bishop sent me here as "a challenge" (a euphemism of church officials). I came here from four years of seminary teaching. Though I had been a pastor for some ten years before going into teaching, Northside gave me the opportunity to learn all over again what it means to be a pastor, a priest to the priests. In this final chapter we shall explore the nature of leadership in the Body of Christ.

In his classic *The Purpose of the Church and Its Ministry*, H. Richard Niebuhr said that, whenever in Christian history there has been a clear, intelligible conception of the ordained ministry, four things were known: what its chief purpose was, what constituted a call to this ministry, the source of the minister's authority, and whom the minister served.[1]

Today, we have been going through a crisis of ministry. Laypersons sometimes complain that their pastors don't act like pastors. Pastors complain that the laity have too many and too diverse expectations for what their pastor is supposed to be doing. Who are ministers, and what are they supposed to be doing?

There has been a frantic search for some attribute that somehow makes pastors unique among Christians. Clergy are said to be "wounded healers" and "living reminders" (Henri Nouwen), "sacramental persons," (Urban Holmes), "symbol bearers," (John Westerhoff), "the clown" (David Switzer).[2] This sort of talk leads one to ask if ministers have anything to do.

One source of confusion is our inadequate ecclesiology. For instance, my own United Methodist *Discipline* says that "pastors are responsible for ministering to the needs of the whole community as well as the needs of the people in their charges."[3] Is it accurate to say that ministers are ordained to serve the world at large? I live in Bible Belt Greenville, yet I have noted that, even here, not all welcome or recognize my authority. If ministers are to be out in the world at large, what does this say to the ministry of other Christians? Are the distinctions between the church and the world so blurred that we can now stop worrying about upbuilding the church and simply do good things for the world at large? The church that I have in mind in these pages is more exclusive than the extravagantly inclusive statement in the *Discipline* indicates.

Why does the church have clergy in the first place? A few years ago, when Pat Boone baptized a number of his friends in the swimming pool at his California home, he justified his actions by saying something to the effect that, wherever a couple of people are gathered in Jesus' name, there is a church, and whenever a person is a Christian, that person is his own priest.

In our rites of ordination, the church designates leaders and tells them what they are to do. The statement in the old Lutheran ordinal is typical:

Ministers of Christ are His ambassadors and as such are to preach the Word and administer the Holy Sacraments. They are appointed to wait upon and serve the Church, which is the bride of Jesus Christ, . . . to offer before Him the prayers and supplications of His people; to feed, to instruct, to watch over, and to guide the sheep and the lambs of His flock, whom He hath purchased with His own blood.

As Luther said, all baptized Christians share the gifts of the Spirit, the command to preach, evangelize, witness, heal, and serve. This is the "priesthood of believers." This does not mean "each person is his or her own priest" but "each person is his or her neighbor's priest." The First Epistle of Peter is addressing all the church, not just the clergy, when it says to newly baptized Christians:

But you are a chosen race, a royal priesthood, a holy nation, God's own people, that you may declare the wonderful deeds of him who called you out of darkness into his marvelous light. Once you were no people but now you are God's people; once you had not received mercy but now you have received mercy. (1 Peter 2:9–10)

This is the church's mandate for ministry. All Christians share it. Yet, from the earliest stirrings of the church, some Christians were designated for the task of equipping the saints, caring for the church, upbuilding the community, and representing the church as a whole. Ordination puts some Christians under orders, making them officials, community persons.

And his gifts were that some should be apostles, some prophets, some evangelists, some pastors and teachers, to equip the saints for the work of ministry, for building up the body of Christ. (Eph. 4:11–12)

Priests are officials of the church. The pastoral ministry is a species of a broader genus called ministry. The church has pastors and priests as a function of the church's mission. Pastors exist because of certain things that need doing in the church.

In his criticism of the medieval priesthood, Luther said that the church sometimes acts as if priests are the only Christians who are called to witness, to serve, to heal. Throughout the history of the church, there is a recurring tendency to take those gifts, graces, and duties that are part of every Christian's baptismal inheritance and give these to the ordained Christians alone.

Against medieval definitions of the priesthood, the Reformers asserted that the essence of the clergy is not in some indelible character conferred at ordination. Clergy are "special" only because they are officials. They are not some upper crust set over the lowly laity. The essence of the ordained ministry is essentially relational (whom it serves) and functional (what it does), not ontological (what it is).

Very little is said about these officals in the New Testament. Probably the ordained ministry arose quite spontaneously in the church, the way leadership emerges spontaneously in any human group, particularly in those human groups that try to do something important. The ordained priesthood arises from "below," from the church's very mundane need for leadership. At the same time, it arises from "above," as a "gift of the Lord" (Eph. 4:8–11; 1 Tim. 4:14), a Lord who will not let his people be without the gifts they need to fulfill their mission. Perhaps the church was surprised that, even in these later days, God still called leaders for his people, even as Moses was called to lead from slavery, even as the prophets were called to speak the truth.

All this is to say that the ordained ministry is not a status. It is a function. This cannot be said too strongly, because when people talk about clergy, they cannot resist searching for some peculiar, special attribute that belongs only to pastors and thus legitimates their existence: wounded healer, living reminder, clown, poet, empathetic listener, goal setter, enabler, guru, celibate, prayer virtuoso, or some other individual natural or acquired trait that somehow makes a priest "special." This implies that the church's need for leadership, service, and edification is not special enough, that the church's calling of its leaders needs something else added to it for it to be holy.

Earlier in this book, we took a rather mundane, earthly, functional view of the church, noting that it was the communal, bodily, corporeal nature of the church that caused people problems. The same can be said for the ordained ministry. The essence of the pastoral ministry is its functionality, its service to the Body, its work as a community official.

Ask yourself: What is the difference between a pastor visiting, preaching, baptizing, and any other Christian doing these jobs? The essential difference is in the "officialness." I have a dozen laypeople at Northside who read Scripture aloud in Sunday worship better than I. I've got four dozen who visit elderly shut-ins better than I. The difference is that when I do these things, I do them as the "community person," with the authorization of the whole church.

When a pastor visits, teaches, preaches, baptizes, the church "reads" his or her actions different from the same actions done by unordained Christians. The pastor bears the burden of our tradition, the obligation to represent the whole church through all ages, the responsibility to edify the whole Body, to keep us together in the church.

Those of us who are pastors are community persons, officials of the church. Certainly the pastor, like any other Christian, must walk the journey of faith personally. But ordination impels the pastor to walk with the whole church in mind.

Historically, whenever the church has forgotten the corporate, ecclesial, functional origins of the ordained ministry, problems have developed. For instance, in the Middle Ages, as tension between the church and the world relaxed, monasticism became a kind of second baptism, a way to take more seriously one's call to discipleship. Monks were viewed as ideal Christians. Gregorian reform then modeled the parish clergy as resident monks—celibate, set apart, totally devoted holy men who temporarily resided in a congregation. Earlier, the Council of Chalcedon had condemned "absolute ordination," the notion that priests exist apart from a congregation. But by the late Middle Ages, free-lance, roving, monkish clergy at large set the tone for all clergy. The essential linkage between priests and parishes had been severed.

Then there was talk of a priestly "state of grace"—it's a "state" now, not an office. Ministers were said to have an indelible character, stamped upon them in ordination. Once a person was stamped with that character, it couldn't be erased. "Priest forever," was how it was described. Ordination had become a personal possession, a holy power. Ministers were called "little Christs," divine mediators through whom grace trickled down to the lowly laity. This notion of priests as "little Christs" had disasterous consequences in the Vatican's recent argument against women priests. Is the essential basis for ministry a question of who most resembles Christ, or who best serves Christ's church?

Can you see why I am concerned that two of the most popular writers on ministerial spirituality today are Henri Nouwen and Thomas Merton? We pastors are community persons, Body people, not monks. We are called to tasks that are ecclesial, relational, functional, and pastoral, not personal, professional, or universal.

The Challenge of the Pastoral Ministry

When the bishop sent me here, he said it would be a "challenge." That is often a euphemism for "impossible situation." That was not the case here, though this place *has* been a challenge. It is a challenge in the same way that any parish is a challenge to a pastor. As I look out upon my flock on Sunday morning, that sea of faces nearly overwhelms me with their hurt, their expectancy, their need. I know their hurt firsthand now. I have been with them, listened to them, stood with them long enough to know them in their depths and heights. How can I presume to serve these people?

I am not a community person, a pastor, by natural inclination. Tell me I have some charismatic flare for leadership. Praise me for the art of my preaching or the empathy of my pastoral care; just let me share myself and pour out my feelings; urge me to become a spiritual virtuoso, but please don't yoke me to the Body—don't marry me to that unruly bride; don't force me to find who I am among those who gather at 435 Summit Drive, Greenville, South Carolina.

Let me free-lance ministry; give me a degree and tell me I'm special; tack up a shingle, set up office hours, and call me a professional; teach me some exotic spiritual gnosis that makes me holy, but don't hold me accountable to the church.

Like many today, I love Jesus. I want to serve him. But he married beneath his station. For me, the real scandal of the ordained ministry, the ultimate stumbling block, the thing I avoid and fear the most, is the church. Like many of you, I set out to serve God and ended up caught among those whom God served.

My problem, my difficulty, as a priest, is that I am yoked to the church. The pastoral ministry is so tough, its demands so great, because it is ministry as a function of the church.

All Christians are called by God to witness wherever they are, to teach, to preach the gospel among their fellows, to work for justice. But pastors are those Christians who are called to upbuild the church. Prayer, Bible reading, meditation, devotional exercises are as essential for pastors as for other Christians. But the ultimate goal of my spiritual formation must be to more fully yoke me to the Body. I am a community person.

The Call

People ask me, from time to time, "How did you get called into the ministry?" No doubt they are curious how someone like me ended up in a place like this. Perhaps they wonder what sort of blinding flash of light, what holy words imprinted across the sky, could call someone into the ordained ministry.

I expect that my response is a bit disappointing. Like them, I got called at my baptism. I share with them the vocation of all Christians but, as part of my baptismal call, I came to feel that I was also called to be a pastor.

I always asked seminarians, when I taught them, "How did

you get here?" Their response? They tell stories of Sunday school teachers, scoutmasters, little old ladies and men, who first led them toward ministry. The testimony of one woman was typical:

I read the Scripture one Sunday as a lay reader. That was all, just read it. After the service a woman came up to me and said, "Dear, you read so well. Your reading of that passage did something to me. You should be a minister."

That's all. There she was, having left a well-paid job, disrupted her family routine, and gone to seminary, all on the basis of a simple, "Dear, you should be a minister." But does the call to ministry ever become more holy, more special? In all ordination rites of the Western church, in the scant but obvious data on the ordained ministry in the New Testament, I hear this simple, mysterious, holy beginning.

Is it enough? Can we trust the call of God to come through such mundane, communal channels? Though we can rejoice at the personal, inner call of someone into the ministry, historically such private, inner calls from Christ have more in common with the call to the monastic life than to the ancient presbyterate. Sometimes we get people in seminary who don't want to be pastors. They have come to seminary wanting to be better Christians. Seminary is probably the last place for that! The purpose of the seminary is to equip those who are called by the community to be community persons.

When I was in seminary James Dittes presented his research on psychological reasons people go into the ministry.[4] According to Dittes, as children, many pastors were what he calls little adults. The "little adult" is the child who is always the classroom monitor when the teacher leaves the room, the school crossing guard, the child who enforces adult values.

The "little adult" may be respected or even admired by other children, but rarely will this child be popular. Dittes's thesis is that "little adults" are attracted to the pastoral ministry. As pastors, they now enforce God's values among wayward adults just as they once enforced adult values upon wayward children.

One student, upon hearing this, blurted out, "You've just demolished my call into the ministry. I thought God called me. You're telling me that my 'call' was little more than my reaction to other people?"

"Has God stopped calling ministers through other people?" asked Dittes.

We are called to leadership in the community of Jesus Christ through community. The call gets no more blinding and significant than that. It comes, not on a mountaintop or in a cornfield, but in the church.

And so Calvin speaks of the "twofold call" to the ministry. God calls, but the church must also call. Wesley distinguished the "inner" from the "outer" call. Take it as you will, the point is that, outside the need of the community, any personal, purely individual call is incomplete.

As I keep close to God's community, I keep close to my vocation, hearing again and again the voice that first bid me say yes. So, as a pastor, I must keep myself close to the Body. I am sure this discipline takes different forms for different pastors, but for me it means disciplining myself to knock on doors and sit down at the kitchen table and visit. I find nothing about pastoral work more distasteful than visitation—and nothing more essential. Why must it always be me making myself available to them?

He kept close to those he came to save, beside them from his baptism in the Jordan to the breaking of bread. He had his lonely times apart, his monastic closet of prayer, but in the crush of the crowd, amid the multitude, at table with them in argument, beside their beds of pain, in prison, on the cross, he becomes the model for ministry, pastoral and otherwise.

Some mornings, just to keep things in focus, amid opening mail and planning meetings, answering the telephone and worrying about the budget, I walk into the sanctuary at Northside, I envision myself doing those tasks that remind me who I am.

On Sunday, in the pulpit, looking out on this sea of need and promise that I call my congregation, behind the table, setting the meal for the faithful, I find myself doing explicitly what in other pastoral activities often remains implicit and inferred. Here is where my vocation is made visible, ecclesial.

The first stirrings of the ordained ministry in the New Testament are tied to service at the church's liturgical assembly. Even Paul's apostolate was *diakonia,* service, not authority (2 Cor. 1:24; 1 Cor. 3:5; Rom. 11:13). The church has leaders as any other human grouping does—but not as the world conceives of leadership. "It shall not be so [as it is among worldly leaders] among you" (Mark 10:42 f.). We are to lead our people, not by "domineering over those in your flock," says 1 Peter, "but by being examples to the flock" (1 Pet. 5:3).

The First Epistle of Peter (2:9–10) reminds us that it is the *laos,* the people, who are called priests, kings, royalty, holy. The clergy are to be servants of the priests, not the people servants of the clergy. A sacerdotal clergy desacralizes everybody else. If we can get some "professional" for a minister, why would anyone else in the church want to minister? We clergy are always deacons—butler, waiter, servant.

In this strange kingdom, leaders wait upon tables, serve others, wash feet, act foolish, build up others, summon others to a faith that is always social, ecclesial, corporate.

It gets hard out there. I have served some of the best churches any minister could ask for, but the tasks of truth telling, pastoral care, Body building are difficult. The way we pastors keep going is by remembering who chose us, who named us, who ordered us into this cruciform faith.

I get discouraged, confused by the myriad of demands and temptations in the church. But I give thanks that ministry need not be self-sustained. My job is to think about God and God's people. Fortunately, God's self-assigned job is to think about me. So I cling to my vocation. I am reminded of those most hopeful words in all the New Testament: "You didn't choose me, I chose you." I thank God it's not a profession but a vocation.

In a field education seminar at Duke Divinity School, a young man recounted an episode in a hospital room with an old woman dying of cancer. He had been at the church only two weeks, and "I was a bit anxious about my first terminal patient," he said.

One morning she said, "Preacher, I want you to pray for me." He tensed up. Prayer. Well, he thought, I haven't solved all my unanswered questions about prayer. I'm not too sure.

"What would you like me to pray for?" he asked.

"I'd like you to pray that I'll be healed, of course," she said. "Failing that, I want you to pray that I won't suffer if I'm not healed."

Oh no, he thought, faith healing. It's come to that. What can I say? How can I keep my integrity? He hoped a nurse would appear so that he could exit.

"But, but, I'm just not too sure about what I believe about prayer," he said.

"Not sure, eh?" she said. "Well, we're sure, so you just close your eyes and hold my hand and pray. You'll get the hang of it."

And he, Duke-educated, attractive, smart ("could have been a lawyer"), closed his eyes and held that old lady's frail hand and prayed.

"You know," he said, "she was helped. I could see it. Something happened in spite of me"—in spite of me.

And it was then, I think, that the bishop laid on hands, and the church stood and sang *"Veni, Creator, Spiritus,"* and thereby the church made, and God gave, a new pastor.

So I said to that young man, "Someday, at some depressed little church or worse, some big, successful church, you're going to need to remember how you got here. You're going to have to be a pastor even when you don't feel like it, even when you haven't got it all together for yourself. You're going to need to remember who called you into this ministry and why—someday you'll need to remember. So don't forget that little old lady who helped ordain you."

Now to him who by the power at work within us is able to do far more abundantly than all that we ask or think, to him be glory in the church and in Christ Jesus to all generations, for ever and ever. Amen. (Eph. 3:20–21).

Epilogue

IT IS Sunday morning, first day of the week, first day when the reality of the past week's tragedy had begun to sink in. Early, while it was still quite dark, two women walked toward the city cemetery. Making their way through this somber place of death and decay, they at last stood before the tomb where, on last Friday, they had laid to rest their good friend, Jesus.

They, like the other disciples, had hoped that Jesus was the one to redeem Israel. They had hoped that Jesus would take charge, expel the occupying Romans, and set things right. They had hoped. Now, there was no hope as they shivered in the cold dark of this place of death.

Then, the earth shook, the heavens opened, the stone rolled from the door of his tomb. An angel said to the women, "Do not be afraid; for I know that you seek Jesus who was crucified. He is not here; for he has risen, as he said. Come, see the place where he lay. Then go quickly and tell his disciples that he has risen from the dead, and behold, he is going before you to Galilee" (Matt. 28:5–7).

In this experience of the risen Christ, and others, the church was born. The church is the response to the presence of Christ in the world, the result of his having been released into our future. As Karl Barth says, the church lives between the times, between the forty days after the Resurrection and the final return of Christ in glory.[1] This time is the time of the church, the gift of God who does not simply speak a final word over creation and then end it all but waits upon humanity's response. It is the special mission of the church to be part of human responsiveness to the work and word of God in Christ. The church is born from that original charge to "go quickly and tell . . . that he has risen from the dead . . . he is going before you" (Matt. 28:7)

In fact, when you think about it, the only thing different about the world before and after that first Easter morning is the church. It certainly seemed like the same world. The same sun still rose in the east that Sunday. The same Caesar crawled out of bed, yawned, scratched his sides, and called for his slippers. The same people set up their shops in the streets of Jerusalem and hung their wares for people to see. Beggars took their same street corners. And yet, everything had changed.

In this tired old decaying world, a little group of people were gathering. The breathless women were telling their story. Jesus stood in the midst of them and they worshiped (Matt. 28:9). Here, in this gathering of ordinary men and women, with the same, ordinary doubts and fears of anybody who is placed in that situation, they worshiped. In fact, fear is mentioned again and again as their predominant ecclesial emotion. It is a fearful thing, the Bible says, to fall into the hands of the living God.

Now, the church is the first fruits of the Spirit (Rom. 8:23), the down payment for what God promises to do for the whole world (2 Cor. 1:22; 5:5). The meals that the church eats together are a foretaste of the great banquet at the end of the age, that day when the dwelling of God is with men." He will dwell with them, and they shall be his people, and God himself will be with them" (Rev. 21:3). On that day, what happens to the church on Sunday will be so forever.

The church was born with the end-of-time proclamation of Jesus to his disciples. After that Easter morning at the cemetery, history has ended. Yet, history did not end immediately, in spite of what the church thought. So the church must wait. The institutional church as we know it is the result of the church having had to wait. There is thus a permanent tension between the church as a historical institution and the church as an end-of-time eschatological gathering. The church is stretched between this paradox. Where the Easter shock is dulled, the church is in danger of becoming a reactionary force, another human organization trying to live for and to preserve itself. Keep the machinery oiled, the mimeograph machine spitting out programs, and take care that everything is in place.

On the other hand, when the church is filled with the apocalyptic spirit and focuses only upon the end time, it fails to take visible form within social structures, it becomes a thing so detached from the world and history as to be ineffective and disembodied. Without a healthy appreciation for the power of culture, we become the victims of culture. Historically, those communities that see themselves as the most prophetic and spiritual often become a mirror of the culture that they presume to be detached from. Jim Jones's "People's Church" sought to be an enclave isolated from culture and became this culture's most devastatingly violent expression. The question for Jesus' disciples is not, Will we have a body? but rather, Will our body be Christ's?

The paradoxical quality of the church means that we ought to pray for perseverance, endurance, and vision. We must ask for the vision to see how the church is not what it ought to be as well as for the vision to see the church taking form in the midst of us. Though the message of the church is one of the end of time and of history, we must speak that message in our time and place. The Easter shock that calls forth the church transcends the present, pronounces judgment upon the current church, and imparts power to free the church from itself. The church has power only by knowing that its power is beyond itself. The very Spirit that forms the church breaks the church out of itself.

So the church is the community of the Resurrection, the Sunday people who were formed by a surprise and who are still willing to be surprised, always to be reformed and radically recreated. The church is the paradoxical people who can retain their continuity with their origins only by letting go. This is what the church means by its talk of being "in, but not of, the world." It is tough to be this people, to be in the world, speaking to the world, yet not to be captured by the world.

For better or worse, the church is the form that the risen Christ has chosen to take in the world. We exist here as a colony, an advance token of the world that shall be. The mission of the church is to be a resurrected community and then to invite all to participate with us in the surprise of a God who is for us, one of us. The main difference between those of us on the inside of the church and those on the outside is the simple fact that we have heard something whereas they have not. We are not necessarily better than they. We are probably not more intelligent. We are simply those who have heard what the women said that first Sunday morning, have experienced Christ's presence for ourselves, standing among us on Sunday, with us. Yes, like those first Easter people, it can be said of us that "they worshiped him; but some doubted" (Matt. 28:17). Every time we gather, some of us worship, some are afraid, some doubt.

Then, he comes and stands among us, where two or three are gathered in his name, and speaks to us,

All authority in heaven and on earth has been given to me. Go therefore and make disciples of all nations, baptizing them in the name of the Father and of the Son and of the Holy Spirit, teaching them to observe all that I have commanded you; and lo, I am with you always, to the close of the age (Matt. 28:18).

Notes

Chapter 1: Where Is the Church?

1. Paul Minear, *Images of the Church in the New Testament* (Philadelphia: Westminster Press, 1960).
2. Paul Minear, "Church," *Interpreter's Dictionary of the Bible*, vol. I, p. 617.
3. Anne Freemantle, ed. "On the Unity of the Catholic Church" *A Treasury of Early Christianity* (New York: Viking Press, 1953).
4. Vatican I, 1869–70, chap. 7, N.R., 365.
5. Gibson Winter, *The Suburban Captivity of the Churches* (Garden City, N.Y.: Doubleday, 1961).
6. Peter L. Berger, *The Noise of Solemn Assemblies* (Garden City, N.Y.: Doubleday, 1961).
7. Emil Brunner, *The Misunderstanding of the Church* (London: Lutterworth, 1952).
8. C. S. Lewis, *The Screwtape Letters* (New York: Macmillan, 1962), pp. 15–16.
9. Thomas Luckmann, *The Invisible Religion* (New York: Macmillan, 1967).
10. David H. C. Read, *Overheard* (Nashville: Abingdon Press, 1969), pp. 139–40.
11. Dietrich Bonhoeffer, *Life Together*, trans. J. W. Doberstein, (New York: Harper & Brothers, 1954;), pp. 27–28.
12. Karl Barth, *Dogmatics in Outline*, trans. G. T. Thomson (New York: Harper Torchbooks, 1959), pp. 142–143.
13. Bonhoeffer, *Life Together*, p. 30.

Chapter 2: Why the Church?

1. H. E. Nichol, "We've a Story to Tell the Nations," Hymn Number 410 in *The Methodist Book of Hymns* (Nashville: Methodist Publishing House, 1966).
2. James M. Gustafson, *Treasure in Earthen Vessels* (New York: Harper & Row, 1961).
3. H. Richard Niebuhr, *The Purpose of the Church and Its Ministry* (New York: Harper & Row, 1956), pp. 27f.
4. Peter Berger and Thomas Luckmann, *The Social Construction of Reality* (Garden City, N.Y.: Doubleday, 1966), p. 158.
5. C. S. Lewis, *The Screwtape Letters* (New York: Macmillan, 1962), p. 16.
6. Thomas C. Oden, *Agenda for Theology* (New York: Harper & Row, 1979), pp. 128–29.
7. Quoted in Peter Nichols, *Politics of the Vatican* (New York: Praeger, 1968), p. 109.
8. Bonhoeffer, *Life Together*, trans., J. W. Doberstein (New York: Harper & Brothers, 1954), p. 30.

Chapter 3: In, But Not of, the World

1. Peter DeVries, *The Mackerel Plaza* (New York: Popular Library, 1977), pp. 8–9.
2. Will Campbell, *Brother to a Dragon Fly* (New York: Continuum, 1980), pp. 219–220.
3. Richard G. Hutcheson, Jr., "Would the Real Christian Program Please Stand Up?" *The Christian Century* 98 (Oct. 7, 1981), pp. 994–997.
4. Jürgen Moltmann, "Christian Theology Today," *New World Outlook* 62 (1972), pp. 483–90.
5. Stanley Hauerwas, *A Community of Character* (Notre Dame, Indiana: University of Notre Dame Press, 1981), pp. 72–88.
6. Stanley Hauerwas, *Vision and Virtue* (Notre Dame, Indiana: Fides/Clarentian, 1974), p. 52.
7. E. Glenn Hinson, *The Evangelization of the Roman Empire* (Macon, Georgia: Mercer University Press, 1981).
8. Hans Küng, *The Church* (Garden City, N.Y.: Doubleday, 1976), p. 438.
9. Jim Wallis, *Call to Conversion* (New York: Harper & Row, 1982), p. 109.
10. "Letter to Diognetus," *Early Christian Fathers, The Library of Christian Classics*, vol. I, trans. and ed. Cyril C. Richardson (Philadelphia: Westminster Press, 1953), pp. 216–18, italics added.

Chapter 4: Acting Like Christians

1. Iris Murdoch, "Vision and Choice in Morality," in Ian T. Ramsey, ed., *Christian Ethics and Contemporary Philosophy* (London: Routledge & Kegan Paul, 1970), pp. 37f.

Chapter 7: Common Prayer

1. Bard Thompson, ed., *Liturgies of the Western Church* (Cleveland: World, Meridian Books, 1962), p. 8.

Chapter 8: Priests Everywhere

1. H. Richard Niebuhr, *The Purpose of the Church and Its Ministry* (New York: Harper & Row, 1956), p. 58.
2. Henri Nouwen, *The Wounded Healer* (Garden City, N.Y.: Doubleday, 1979); *The Living Reminder* (New York: Seabury, 1981); Urban T. Holmes, *The Future Shape of Ministry* (New York: Seabury, 1971); David K. Switzer, *Pastor, Preacher, Person* (Nashville: Abingdon Press, 1979).
3. Par. 350, *The Book of Discipline* (Nashville: The United Methodist Publishing House, 1972), p. 168.
4. James E. Dittes, *Minister on the Spot* (Philadelphia: Pilgrim Press, 1970), pp. 130–35.

Epilogue

1. John McTavish, Harold Wells, eds., *Preaching Through the Christian Year* (Grand Rapids, MI: Eerdmans, 1979), pp. 210–212.

Index

Abstraction, 8–13, 21
Africa, 72
Apocalyptic, 139
Aristotle, 83
Augsburg Confession, 10
Augustine, 87, 102

Baptism, 23–24, 35, 102, 127, 140
Baptist, 14, 120
Barth, K., 5, 22, 27, 137, 141n
Berger, P., 17, 141n
Body of Christ, 10, 18–21, 24, 28–32, 46–47, 128, 139
Bonhoeffer, D., 25–26, 31, 141n
Bride of Christ, 28–31
Brunner, E., 16, 18–19, 141n
Bultmann, 16

Call. See Vocation
Calvin, J., 10, 40, 43, 133
Campbell, W., 53–54
Catherine of Sienna, 101, 142n
Central Church, 49–74
Christ Church, 75–91
Clergy, 125–136
Colony of Heaven, 37, 40, 64
Council of Chalcedon, 129
Criticism of the Church, 24–25
Cyprian, 9, 13

Devil, 118
DeVries, P., 50–51, 142n
Didache, 69
Diognetus, Letter to, 142n
Dittes, J., 132–133, 142n
Docetism, 19–20, 25, 29, 31, 37

Easter. See Resurrection
Ethics, 75–91
Eucharist. See Lord's Supper

Evangelicals, 14, 89–90
Evangelism, 70
Finney, C. G., 14–15
Fundamentalism, 93, 98

Gogarten, F., 16
Goya, 12
Gustafson, J. M., 37, 141n

Hauerwas, S., 58, 67–68, 142n
Helwig, M., 68
Hinson, G., 69, 142n
Holmes, U., 126, 142n
Hutcheson, R. G., 142n

Incarnation, 10, 20, 29, 32

Jackson, J., 101
James, W., 36–37
John XXIII, Pope, 48

Kant, E., 80–81
Keck, L., 106
Kierkegaard, S., 69
King, M. L., 66
Kung, H., 5, 70–71, 142n

Lewis, C. S., 20, 39–40, 141n
Liberal, 15–16, 54–60, 70–71, 79, 93–98
Loisy, A., 27
Lord's Supper, 45, 102, 114
Luckmann, T., 21, 141n
Lutheran, 10–11, 40, 62, 86, 126–127

Main Street Church, 33–36, 43
McTavish, J., 142n
Marty, M., 54–58
Merton, T., 130
Methodists, 14, 58, 59, 126, 142n

Middle Ages, 9
Minear, P., 10–11, 141n
Moltmann, J., 142n
Moody, D. L., 14–15
Morality. *See* Ethics
Moral Majority, 55, 57
Moravian, 14
Murdoch, I., 142n

Nichol, H. E., 141n
Nichols, P., 141n
Niebuhr, Reinhold, 17
Niebuhr, Richard, 37, 125, 141n, 142n
Niles, D. T., 105
Noah, 94–97, 99–100, 102
Nouwen, H., 126, 130, 142n
Nygren, A., 10

Olden, T., 40, 141n
Ordination, 125–136

Pastoral ministry, 6, 125
Paul, 5, 22, 36, 41, 60, 102, 134
Pentecost, 104–105
Peter, 104–105
Pietism, 14, 81
Poverty, 117–121, 124
Preaching, 101–113, 131
Presbyterian, 14
Priesthood of believers, 127

Quakers, 27

Racism, 110
Rahner, K., 17, 26

Read, David H. C., 23, 141n
Resurrection, 46, 137–140
Revivalism, 14–15
Ritual, 39–40, 122

Salvation, 21–24, 26–27
Schaller, L., 58
Sermons. *See* Preaching
Sheldon, C., 61
Shillebeeckx, E., 5
Social Concern, 49–74
Southey, R., 3
Spencer, P. J., 14
Spirit, 27, 30, 48, 122–123, 138–139, 140
Story, 98–100, 101
Switzer, D., 126, 142n

Television, 103–104
Tertullian, 38
Thielicke, H., 105
Thompson, B., 142n
Tillich, P., 17, 26

Vatican I, 13
Vision, 38–39, 84–85, 98–99, 120–12
Vocation, 131–136

Wallis, J., 55, 71–72, 142n
Wesley, J., 40, 122, 133
Westerhoff, J., 126
Wilder, T., 61
Winter, Gibson, 17, 141n
Worship, 114–117, 121–124. *See also* Baptism, Lord's Supper